Morning Practice for Radiant Humans

Meditations on Finding Our Way Home

by

Dr. Kristin Shepherd

Copyright © by Dr. Kristin Shepherd
ISBN-13 978-1516986378
All rights reserved.
Cover design and text: copyright © 2015 by Dr. Kristin Shepherd

For more information, contact:
Dr Kristin Shepherd on Facebook
or
kristinshepherd.ca

Introduction

This is a simple collection of daily meditations (they feel like conversations to me) on finding our way home. By home, I mean our deepest, truest, most beautiful, original divinity. (If 'divinity' is a word that pisses you off, please stroke it out with a blunt black marker and write 'truth' or 'essence' beside it. It is SO not worth getting our squirrelly ego nuts in a knot over a contentious word at this early stage. Better just to assume your preferences are best, substitute your own language and carry on.)
This conversation is in no way intended as advice or coaching. I'm not interested in that role and I suspect that the best life comes from each of us listening to our own internal guidance.
Like a happy lunatic, I rave about and point toward something beautiful, often invisible, and mostly indescribable. If these ravings resonate with something in you, then you'll feel it in your gut, your heart. You'll listen because you know this is true for you, not because you're missing something or need to be fixed in any way. In this way, you find your own way home.
My own leanings toward this come from a history in health care. I was a chiropractor for twenty years, during which time it became evident that our head and heart narratives become our physical narratives. Over

time, it seemed the natural thing to do, even for improved health, was focus on the best possible narratives. (These days I write for theatre and film, with a focus on finding love in difficult circumstances.)

My experience is that some kind of morning practice - meditation, quiet breathing, appreciation, wonder, being here, now, remembering who we are, shifting focus toward openness, love, forgiveness, compassion, and courage - creates a different day, a different body, and a different life. Literally. From the moment I finish a morning practice, I experience a different world, one that is more generous, more passionate, more loving, more connected. I become an agent of peace, presence, and forgiveness - still a human ass with an idiotic ego some days, but over time I'm remembering more often and more clearly.

My guess is that a morning practice allows us to recognize a truer version of ourselves.

If we speak about this in terms of energy or vibration, it's as though we're always humming some tune.

We're humming with resentment about work or guilt about relationships or despair about the environment or anger about politics, or we're humming with hope, joy, confidence, courage. And whatever we're humming with connects with people and events that are humming the same tune. Angry people hang with angry people. Victims hang with victims. Joy hangs with joy.

One of the huge benefits of a practice is coming to know that we choose the hum. We practice humming the tune we want to live and life shifts in response. It's tough to overstate the difference this makes.

These wee blurbs are the result of my own practice. They seem to write themselves. And it seems they've served a community of readers (I include myself in this community), many of whom have reminded me that they'd like a collected version. I understand the desire, having highlighted, underlined, starred, and corner-folded collections from of Hugh Prather, Wayne Dyer, Pema Chödrön, Thich Nhat Hanh, Abraham Hicks, and all the other human lanterns.

A poet friend once told me it's worth living with writing that moves you, that in living with it, in going over and over that parts that resonate, the writing becomes a part of your literary DNA.
I suspect it goes beyond literary.
My spirit DNA, if there is such a thing, is glad for the reminders.
The idea of collecting these written meditations makes me laugh because it feels as though I'm repeating the same thing every single morning: Look! Remember. Open. Love. Forgive. Be Here, Now. Drop Everything Else. Let The Universe Do Its Job.
So simple, but so important that I'm glad to be tuned by it every day.

The writings are in no particular order except for their alphabetical titles in the hopes that it becomes easy, over time, to find the ones that matter to you.

I note that there are some seasonal writings, holidays having such potential for astronomical insanity. Many of these have 'Christmas' in the title. Please forgive my narrow cultural history and habits. If it's any consolation, the whole Christ/Jesus/BigR thing messes with me until I translate it all as Christ consciousness.

I also note a recurrent squirrel theme, about which I am mystified. Same goes for curious spellings (Canadian) and the overuse of both parentheses and commas.

I hope these pages serve to help you laugh, to be brave, to adore yourself and to adore the rest of the crazy, flawed human (squirrelly!) circus we're a part of.

Mostly, I hope it serves to help you keep the gates of your unique and invaluable heart wide open. That's what the world needs from you.

Thanks to all of you who asked for this,

kristin

Drop Everything

Drop everything you can: every thought, every decision about who you are, every belief, every struggle, every desire, every bit of suffering, every fear, all your history.
Keep dropping and stay right here.
See what remains.
This one practice would be enough.
(This makes me laugh.)

Hope this serves.
Love.

A Prayer To My Weaknesses

Some days, the only thing I can come up with is to send masses of love to my weaknesses. By weaknesses, I mean my stubborn, self-destructive, completely ego-driven habitual thoughts, feelings, and @#%*-ing behaviours. (Excuse the language.) (Maybe that's one of mine.)

My prayer looks like this:

Dearest &%$#-ing fear (of ending up a poverty-stricken, chain-smoking, cat-food-eating, greasy-haired, bitter, morbidly obese, dead-end-dwelling, repulsive, unimaginative infomercial addict - okay that's one of mine, feel free to substitute your own),

I know that you exist. I feel for you, being so afraid. Come into the room for a minute. Sit under the light where we can see each other.

Here's the truth: you're a collection of thoughts, and although it's true that my attention goes back to you over and over as though you matter, you don't. You're a bad habit. Period. You exist because I continue to breathe life into you. You're loud, you're persistent, I'll give you that, but you are a tiny part of my entirety. Feel free to stay in the room.

I'm going to shift my attention toward something more beautiful.

Kindergarten love spends its energy putting out emotional fires. Grown- up love spends its energy discovering the thing that can't burn down.

Hope this serves.
Love.

A Quiet Mind is So Delicious

Stop believing your thoughts so readily.
(I don't have enough love/money/health might account for most of them, and my god, don't we just repeat these day in and day out? Stab me with a fork if we can't find a better internal life than this!)
Most of our thoughts are insane, whacked, nutso, arbitrary, damaging, and certainly smaller than who we really are.
Bring your attention home.
Bring your attention away from your stories.
Come home to your breath.
Find one moment - one moment! - of no-thought.
A quiet mind is so delicious that it'll change your life.

Hope this serves.
Love.

Am I Here?

I get irritated some mornings when my lovely man professes to be present with me in conversation while he's looking at car ads on his laptop in bed. I say, are you with me? And what I mean is, you're not with me, look at me while we're talking.
This cracks me up. Talk about taking someone hostage.
I'm looking for someone to be with.
The solution is for me to be with me.
Am I here? Am I here? Just keep asking until I'm here.
How am I? In my heart, I mean, not in my head. Keep asking until I can feel myself. Until I have breathed myself back into this body.
When is it? When is it? Until I'm here now. Now.
And bingo, I let the hostages go. They can be wherever they want, on their own path for the day. The lovely man can look for cars, the dog can have a nap, the world can go about its business, and I am home.

#theanswerisntoutthereitsinhere

Hope this serves.
Love.

Are You Tired Of Taking Everything So Personally?

Are you tired of taking everything so personally? Your repeated failures, your weeny successes, your character flaws, your absurd-but-sticky fears, your decades-old wounds, the shmuckiness of the shmucks in your life?
Are you tired of taking all of that to heart?
Ahh, that's good to hear.
None of that belongs anywhere near your heart, anyway.
And none of that has anything to do with who we really are.

Lots of love your way.

As Long As I End Up Gorgeous

From Cosmic Laughs, season one, episode one:
I'm all for letting go as long as that means I end up gorgeous, successful, wealthy, popular, and in total control.

Love.

Be An Instrument of Love Today

Fill yourself up, or empty yourself out - pick the one that resonates most with you - and then become an instrument of love.

Meet your own needs for love, dreaming, deserving, and self care, and then you're free to love the ones who need it most.

There is almost nothing better than deciding who to send love to today.

Someone easy, like my kids? (For some, kids are hard, because they can be asses, just like us.) Or the friends who will tell me I'm wonderful when I need to hear it? Or someone more challenging, like the guy who has never seemed to like me, or worse, the old friend who did like me and now is closed. The one whose values make me cringe. The one I don't trust. The drama queen. The cruel one. The cynical one. The one who refuses to admire me. The hugely successful one who pisses me off.

The tough ones get my prideful, resistant ego going. No way I'm going to send love to that bugger, we say. They don't deserve my love. What they need is my disapproval. What they need is a karmic boomerang to the head.

This is the coward's path. (And the coward is only cowardly because she has not loved herself yet.)

The braver thing is to realize that they - the tough ones to love - have nothing to do with this.
They are the excuse I use to walk around with a closed heart, period.
There isn't a being on this planet that doesn't deserve love.
If you believe this, act on it.
There is no situation ever that isn't improved with love.
If you believe this, act on it.
Don't close the gates.

Hope this serves.
Love.

Be Brave. Keep Jumping

"Don't drink at the water's edge. Throw yourself in. Only then will your thirst be quenched." Jeanette Berson

I used to think I would instantly and effortlessly dissolve into love by embracing these statements, that they would be a kind of miracle cure for my humanness. I hoped for that. Fervently.
I also hoped that dissolving into love would be a pretty process, that letting go of junk would be graceful and lovely. (Think Audrey Hepburn.)
But every day I wake up and am still human. Every day the letting go is a decision. And sometimes the process is ugly and obscenely repetitive.
The "throw yourself in" quotes are still gorgeous. They make me feel courageous and stir up a central, powerful longing for freedom, a kind of recognition of oneness.
They do send me running toward the water, but they also make me laugh, now, because of the human crust that I start out with every single day.
Now I know, I trust, that I am water. I am a drop in the great ocean. In the big picture, I am the great ocean.
But some days it doesn't feel like this.

Some days I feel like a huge, thirsty ciabatta bun lurching on doughy legs toward the deep end of the pool. A crusty, chewy, aromatic, not particularly healthy, completely manufactured being hits the water and becomes a soggy, gross, disgusting, broken down mess. It discovers itself to be flour and air and not much else. It accepts this and decides for the four billionth time to go. It floats until waterlogged and then sinks with a bit of kicking and screaming into the constant, deep end of love.
The point of this lousy analogy is just to say that some days this trip is peaceful and easy. Some days it isn't. Be gentle with yourself for being human.
Even when it's messy, we know that love is where we come from and is where we're headed.
Be brave. Keep jumping.

Hope this serves.
Love.

Be Gentle Toward Addictions

Be gentle toward your addictions and the addictions of others (to control, image, dominance, people pleasing, conflict, sugar, shoes, and booze, to name a few).

At the centre of each of these is a yearning for transcendence, for freedom, for love, for home.

Lots of love your way.

Be The One Who Keeps Your Heart Open No Matter What

Don't let your thoughts or the the thoughts and actions of people around you determine whether your gates are open or closed.
Somebody says something threatening, cold, critical, rejecting? Open your heart to them.
Afraid of your future? Open your heart.
Carrying past junk that hurts? Open your heart toward it.
Why don't we do this automatically?
We close the gates for fear of being run over and flattened. Annihilated.
We create a fortress, don't we? We build it, we defend it, we carry the weight of it. (Don't say this to me or I'll shut you out, don't do that to me or I'm out of here, these are my people, these are not my people, I will not love someone who disagrees with me, I need to fight for my rights or my world will go to hell, I know how this goes because it always goes this way, I need to do x,y, and z to protect myself from a dangerous future, etc.)
We build and build the structure, brick by solid brick. But man, it's cold, dark, and lonely in there after a while. All those walls! And no light.

Drop it. Open the gates every time you feel yourself resisting, defending.
Be hurt. Be scared. Be vulnerable. Be undefended.
Let thoughts, feelings, reactions pass through.
Stop protecting yourself from life.
Be with what life is in this moment and then move on to the next moment without carrying anything.
This is what your energy is designed to do.
This is how we thrive.

#thisisusbecomingradiant

Hope this serves.
Love.

Be Willing to Serve

Be willing to serve.
You don't have to figure out how, you don't have to wrap yourself in a bed sheet and get all Mother Teresa, you don't have to even talk about it.
Just be willing and the universe will take you up on your offer.

Love.

Be Your Own Valentine First

Be your own Valentine first.
Love your face (the "map of my time here" says Laura Smith), love your one-and-only body, love those crazy fears and flaws, love that mind that will not be quiet, love your evolution toward living freely in this moment, love your enormous, courageous, connected heart.
(This is the only way you can be someone else's Valentine without it turning into a tug-of-war that makes us both feel less free, less whole.)
Be the one that loves you no matter what.

Hope this serves.
Love to you.

Beautiful Humans: My Dad

We stop so that I can retie his shoelace on the way into the medical building. A year ago he wouldn't have let me. Six months ago he wouldn't have let me.
The tests are hard to watch.
I used to be bright, he tells the gerontologist as he struggles to scrawl a tiny spiral of numbers on the clock face. The damned clock test, we call it.
He gets the day wrong, the month wrong, but the season right after much thought. Watching him, I'm aware of how complicated this question about the season is. It's mid-March. Winter is ending, spring is close but not quite here, and there's no evidence of any of that in this office. How does he get this one right?
At home, he's been practicing for today's tests by memorizing short lists. Apple, penny, honesty. Five minutes into the interview, he remembers apple but not the others. I'm so relieved for him, and proud, getting apple. I spend half the appointment trying not to cry.
He remembers his degrees except for the honorary ones. He remembers his first career in the U.K. but doesn't recall having been the chairman of the Science Council of Canada or that he started an electronics company that employed half the town where I grew up.

So you're bright, says the gerontologist when we fill in some of the holes in my dad's history.

I used to be bright, says my dad.

There's a big difference between being bright and being able to remember, says the gerontologist. You're still bright.

I could kiss this guy's feet after all the medical doctors who have treated my dad like a gaping hole in the room: doing their best, I'm sure, too hurried to connect, too clever by half (my dad would have said), careless with diagnosis and casually prescribing drugs that make him worse or turn out to be useless. Insisting, visit after visit, that respite care and home care are available when needed during precipitous bouts of dementia. In fact, the doctors see the system one way, the CCAC sees it differently, and the retirement homes see it differently again. Here's what should be available, here's what is available, here's the timeline that leaves him stranded. Three contradictory stories every time we make the rounds, and we cobble together half-assed solutions somewhere in the middle of it all.

Still, today is good. We get what sounds like a more accurate diagnosis of Lewy Body Disease. It comes with new drugs and a very strong suggestion that we'll see improvements in my dad's pain control, his nighttime delusions, and his fluctuating memory loss over the next six weeks. Improved quality of life for the immediate future.

My father's wife is not comforted. She's the one who cares for him and watches their life shrink from day to day. Her friend's husband recently died from this Lewy Body disease. It wasn't pretty, she says.
My dad and I become annoyingly cheerful about his shiny future. We celebrate together at lunch. He shakes his tiny fist in the air.
I drive back to my own city, feeling lucky to be close enough to help. He is the reason I'm alive at all and I'm only now old enough to absorb this.
The next day, I get word that he's dizzy and struggling to put sentences together.
I remember that I was going to massage his neck while I was there. He has horrendous neck pain and only recently has begun to let me touch him. It's more physical contact than we've had ever. He mentioned when I arrived this time that he'd just read that physical touch may be essential in dementia care. I couldn't believe he could say this. This admission of want and need is completely new.
And I forgot to do it, somehow. Damn, damn.
This is ageing. This is my dad. This is his last lap, his straightaway. This is me, tying his shoelaces as he shuffles toward the finish.
All I can do is make sure it's a love story.

Hope this serves.
Love.

Becoming Less of a Dickhead

There's nothing lofty about this morning practice of being here, now.
It's just helpful in a very human, practical way.
Through it, I become less ruled by ego, so that I become less of a dickhead when threatened.
Through practice, I am threatened less and threatened less often by the raising of someone's eyebrow, a tight tone of voice, and the kabillion forms of (perceived) rejection of my work, my body, my choices.
I begin to see (like light coming through a crack in the door) that your reaction to me has more to do with your own challenges today, your own constricted heart.
Through practice I meet other flawed humans with compassion. I'm more likely to ask myself, have I ever been an idiot? Afraid? Cynical? Bullying? Mistaken? Yes?
Well then, let this hostage go. He's just another sweet heart doing his best to find his way home.
Through practice I remember to see the sky, taste my coffee, feel the softness of my dogwog's hair when she comes to demand a walk outside.
Through practice, I realize all is good.
We make this choice every day.

#shiftthinkingshiftfeeling

Hope this serves.
Love.

Behind All Lousy Behaviour

There is some suffering, some separation from love, behind all lousy behaviour.
Inside is an innocent kid unable to find her/his way home.
See this.
Compassion is the only sane response.
(The other guy isn't making me nuts. My lack of compassion is what's really making me nuts. I have used someone else's suffering as an excuse to turn off my heart. THIS is nuts.)

Hope this serves.
Love.

Being Here, Now, Is a Huge, Active, Radical Choice

"Acceptance looks like a passive state, but in reality it brings something entirely new into this world. That peace, a subtle energy vibration, is consciousness."
Eckhart Tolle

I love this. We have a Western culture thing that makes a lot of this consciousness stuff look like lazy resignation, as though it's nobler and smarter to be fighting against something, pushing our way to somewhere, getting up and doing what we don't want to get somewhere we want to go.
Being fully here, now is a huge, active, radical choice. Be here. Look someone in the eye. Look yourself in the eye. Breathe fully.

#thisisitthisisitthisisit

Hope this serves.
Love.

Being Willing To Listen

Once in a while (okay, almost every morning), I need to remind myself to open my mind, open my heart, open my body, open my cells, open my energy.
Then gratitude comes more easily. So does forgiveness. So does trust. So does a peaceful mind.
This gets easier with practice, but I still need to make the choice.
(It's not so hard to choose. Something calls, so it's more like being willing to listen.)

Hope this serves.
Love.

Bow To Love

In this culture, we scoff at the idea of bowing down before our divinity, the infinite, truth, love, freedom. The idea of divinity, of surrender, of throwing ourselves at the feet of the unknown, looks lunatic, dangerous, irresponsible, unscientific, irrational.
Consider two things:
We refuse to surrender the supremacy of the thinking mind, believing that my mind is the centre of who I am.
Is this true? This mind - the one that changes with mood, circumstances, weather, medication, media - is this the absolute centre of your being?
Or do you sense something truer, deeper?
Would it not be interesting to look? Would I not have to surrender my certainty about my mind's supremacy in order to look?
Also, isn't it true that we do indeed bow down, that we surrender every day to our fears about security, success and failure, rejection, poverty, illness, etc-blah-blah-etc?
If it's true that we are surrendering to that junk,
maybe it's time to make more conscious choices about where we're bowing.
Bow to truth, bow to freedom, bow to love.

Hope this serves.

Love.

Bring Your Attention to Right Now

For a moment, bring your attention from yesterday or later today to right now.
Bring your attention into this room. The colour on the walls, the sounds. Smells. (Wow. Nice temperature. Fresh air. Didn't notice that until now.)
Then bring your attention to your body. Smell what is, feel the air on your skin, hear your breath, feel your breath.
Then bring attention inside your body.
To the alive-ness here. This is more subtle.
Stay here for a bit.
This inward-moving process may make a part of you restless, impatient, and nuts. Tasmanian devil in a bag.
This is ego and egos do this. No big deal.
It makes a truer level of you light, relieved, and happy.
Quiet.
Like you're finally home.
Pay attention to this one.

Hope this serves.
Love.

Christmas - Holidays and Family

'Tis the season to be insane.
Go ahead, be insane, but have a sense of humour about it.
Remember that who you really are has very little to do with malls, mainlining sugar, traditional anything, what the kids expect, what you expect from your kids, what the parents expect, what your spouse should know or do, drunken relatives, big R religion, spending your way into black holes, time off or not off, driving madly across provinces/states to make everybody happy, or feeling strange because you're alone.

It's a farce. Step back, observe, laugh, and remember who you are.
#hohoho

Hope this serves.
Love.

Christmas - 'Tis The Season

'Tis the season to be driven mad by nutso material standards and nutso family interactions, not to mention whacks of sugar and this expectation that you must feel good will toward all shmucks throughout.

I was in a health care practice for a long time and was astounded by the number of people, including religious leaders, who became depressed as hell during this season.
I get it. Completely.
Yes, it's a crazy time.
It's also a gorgeous opportunity to remember that NONE of this has anything to do with who we really are.
Who I really am can't be offended. My ego can. What a fantastic chance to understand this again!
Who I really am doesn't need to make anyone happy.
Who I really am can wander around malls or not.
Who I really am is enormous and open.
When I remember this, life flows through without resistance.
It all becomes a love fest.
And when it gets gnarly, when I forget, I say, Oh! There I go again, being human!

I look into someone's eyes, or I breathe, or I let my face soften. I remember goodness. Maybe I remember to laugh.
And fall back into my openness.

#hohopractices
#rememberingwhoweare

Hope this serves.
Love

Christmas - Delirious Love

If, during this mad season, you have moments of delirious love for the crowd, that knowing that the bad driver is me and I am that crabby librarian, I am the sloppy drunken uncle, I am the compulsive shopper, the bulimic, the bitter ex, the guy I gave a loonie to on University Ave who looked so deeply into my eyes the other day, I am the one who feels loved and the one who feels left out and out of step with festive everything, I am the one being born and the one who passed away this year--
If you feel these flashes of oneness, throw yourself into them. They are the truth. Come let us adore them, joy to the world, and all of that.
Be dorky with love. (Let the cynics laugh. We are one with them, too.)
Allow yourself to be unhinged by love.
What a present to give yourself.

Hope this serves.
Love.

Christmas - No Presents, Just Singing

In my immediate family (two exceptionally wonderful adult kids, lovely man, and Rosie the dog), we don't do presents.
It's my rule. It's my handicap, maybe, but nothing sucks the joy out of a beautiful day like contemplating malls and crowds and buying or receiving STUFF.
We sing. This is the biggest deal. (My daughter's rule is no one sings, not even warmups, until she gets there.)
We play word games and charades.
We eat a few organized meals.
We freak out about the days getting longer.
It's enough. More than enough. It's perfect.
I hope you're doing what makes you happiest this season, whether it's shopping your face off or wandering in the woods.
And if you find yourself compromising or giving your self away a little bit by doing what doesn't feel perfect, don't despair. Breathe once or twice.
Finding a little oasis of peace, love, and sanity inside the circus tent is a great practice.

Hope this serves.
Love.

Cranky Jags

We get into cranky jags, don't we? Into a habit of being cranky with certain people or situations.

You're always justified in being pissed off. Let's just assume that this isn't in question. You're right, the other guy is an unethical, immoral, unfeeling bastard buffoon. You have no need to prove that you're the good guy.
The question is, do you feel good being pissed off?
If you do, hang onto your anger, breathe life into it, enjoy it, be lifted and energized by it.
If it doesn't make you feel good (and even if it did for 27 years, it may come to an end), do not go around saying you can't help being pissed off.
That throws your power away. It's also untrue.

If your anger makes you feel lousy, drop it for a second. When it comes up again, drop it again.
This will take practice, but this choice to drop it is yours and yours alone.
Your anger has nothing to do with the other guy.
Your anger is a feeling you have cultivated in your own garden.
(If anger makes you feel good, it's because it's better than the shrivelled, silent despair that preceded it.
This is a healthy stage.

If it feels bad, it's because you're in touch with the love/joy that is your ground, your earth, and you know that chronic anger doesn't belong there.)

Take care of yourself by letting go of everything that isn't as beautiful as you.
A worthy practice over coffee on a Saturday morning.

Hope this serves.
Love

Decide To Look From The Heart

Pointing the way home:
No one ever means you harm. You only see that if your weeny ego is seeing someone else's weeny ego. And you only believe that distorted view if you continue to feed it.
Throw that whole picture out.
Decide to look from your heart. (From there, we're all the same, huge heart.)
This is how we serve.

Lots of love your way.

Deeper, Quieter, Calmer

Your power comes from directing your attention toward what is true and not being distracted by the flickering, superficial stuff in front of your face.
(It's like learning not to stare like a zombie at the TV on the wall in the diner.)
What is true is deeper, quieter, calmer.
Don't take this on faith. Find it.
Find it now by paying attention to your next breath. In that breath, if you sink into it, there is no to-do list, no fear, no disappointment, no illness, no addiction, no need to be loved by anyone else.
Find it by asking who you really are and following that question as it goes deeper and deeper, as it peels away the not-so-true layers of personality.
This is remembering who you are.

Lots of love your way.

Defending The House

Explore your passionate beliefs: rights, wrongs, shoulds.

With these beliefs, a mind builds walls and a structure. It feels good to say, this is who I am, I believe in this, I am this kind of house. (Also, this is how I am different from and in some way better than those other houses.)

And we think, what's the problem with this? I accomplish things, I find my tribe, I make a difference, I feel a sense of purpose, I know who I am.

All of which is great individual ego/personality work. Stay there if it feels great.

For some of us, there are clues that there is an I that is deeper and truer.

Clue: When your beliefs are challenged, do you feel defensive, offensive, angry, hurt, threatened, smarter than, stupider than, depressed, or some other riff on reactive? (How can she not agree with me? Why wasn't he there for me? Ice bucket dumping is good! Bad! Necessary! Harmful! The best thing that ever happened! What kind of parent buys a cell phone for a five year old? Of course yoga is more highly evolved than rugby! You pierced your what?)

Powerful reacting happens if you have started to believe you are the house. You have agreed to and are defending that structural definition of self.
Consider the possibility that you are not the structure, not the walls. You may be exploring them, designing them, even, but you are not the beliefs themselves. Maybe you are the unlimited, full-spectrum energy that flows inside the house, outside the house, through the walls, and everywhere else.
If you sense this is true, there is no need to defend your house. You have no fixed position, so no position to defend.
You can also look at other houses and be curious, entertained, and glad for all the variety in the world.
And you can now be grateful for the bugger who challenges you, pointing the way toward a larger picture of you.

Hope this serves.
Love.

Do Not Feel Guilty For Supporting Your Own Happiness

Funny, how often (and for how many decades!) we can feel guilty for making decisions that support our own happiness.
Especially if that choice is associated with resentment/anger/hurt on someone else's face.
As though it's wrong to choose our own joy!
Let that nonsense go.
You are here for joy, for the management of your OWN energy.
The resentment/anger/hurt of other beautiful humans is their business. They'll manage their way back to joy if they care to.
Be glad that you care enough about yourself and your sanity to choose joy.
Act with good intent and from the heart and stop needing to please every face.
This is clean energy.

Hope this serves.
Love.

Does It Scare You?

Does it scare you to listen to what your heart wants? Does it scare you to speak that truth and act on it? Good for you. If it scares the ego, you're onto something good.

#whoyoureallyareisnotafraid

Love and freedom your way.

Don't Get So Yanked

You win, you lose. The world loves you, the world
doesn't love you. You're up, you're down.
Don't get so yanked by this.
You can't go on inhaling forever.
Breathe in, breathe out.
Life brings you both.
Can you be open to both?

Hope this serves.
Love.

Don't Make a Case For Hanging On

By their nature, feelings come and go.
Don't make a case for hanging on to the ones that make you suffer.
So yeah, anger passes through. But if I start reviewing and replaying the reasons for my anger - the hundreds of things that exist in my world that I wish could be "fixed" - my partner, my health, my career, a thousand global situations - I'm inviting anger to put down roots and grow old with me.
This doesn't mean I need to ignore the world and it doesn't mean not responding in whatever way feels best.
But you don't need to cultivate a relationship with suffering in order to live in the world.
Let it in, let it out.
Like breathing.

Hope this serves.
Lots of love.

Don't Take Your Struggles Too Personally

Don't take your struggles too personally.
Don't staple them to your heart, don't lead with them, don't convince yourself that they define you.
And don't run from them. Instead, invite them in and use them.
They're a reminder to wake up, to remember who you really are.
As soon as you wake up, you see the struggle belongs to a much smaller, thrashing, gnashing, temporarily insane version of you.
Open up and the struggle dissolves.
If it shows up again, open up again.
(Don't get caught thinking, this is useless, it only dissolves it for a moment and then it comes back. It is what you can do in this moment of choice that matters.)
Open and let go. This is a beautiful use of energy.

Hope this serves.
Love.

Don't Get Caught In Your Stories

Don't get caught in your stories: I'm too busy, don't like rush hour traffic, hate it when my work is rejected, nervous about an audition/interview next week, pants are tight, car is making funny sounds again and may not last the year, why have I not been meditating.
These stories are valid and justified.
They're also boring filler, like bad songs running in your head.
Lowest common denominator stuff.
Be aware of this. Wake up. And change your focus.
Be here. Focus on your breath.
Let the stories go.
When it's time to fix the car, you'll know it. You don't need to repeat the story a thousand times in order to do the right thing with the car.
You're in rush hour traffic or you're not. There is no suffering around this until you start repeating a story of suffering in your head.
And worrying about last week or next week does nothing but wreck the present moment. Strangely, wrecking the present moment does nothing to change the past or make next week go any better.
Stories come. Let them. Don't get attached and don't get stuck repeating them.
Let them go.
Be the one noticing all of this.

Be the one choosing.

#findthequietplace

Hope this serves.
Love.

Don't Resist Heartbreak

Don't resist heartbreak. Open to it and through it. Let yourself crack wide open.
Keep opening.
Feel it. There is lots to discover here that might not be discovered without being brought to your knees. Snot is so humbling.
But don't be seduced by it, don't get self-righteous about it. Of course you have the right to hold onto it forever and ever, and it's probably justified and you'll certainly find lots of friends to pain-bond with this way, but who you are is larger than this.
Let it be weather that comes and goes.
Keep opening.
This is not advice. It's an invitation.

Hope it serves.
Love.

Drop The Labels

It's one thing to grieve. It's another to create and maintain an identity of the griever.
It's one thing to help someone. It's another to build and carry the identity of helper.
It's one thing to make a smoothie. It's another to feel you have to be the model of perfect health every day in front of everyone.

Same goes for being 'successful', 'healthy', 'wise', 'compassionate', 'a survivor', the teacher, etc.
If the label makes you feel free and alive, keep it.
But look closely. Labels tend to confine after a brief initial whoosh.
You can feel the difference.
Does it serve you to punctuate your conversations by saying, well, you know me, I'm THIS?
Why reduce your magnificent self this way?
Why not just be here, do whatever you do, and drop the identities?
Lighten up. Drop the labels. See how that feels.
Maybe we can find out what we in each moment.
Maybe every moment can be a discovery.

Hope this serves.
Love.

Drop The Weeny

Knowing I can shift my thoughts and feelings is hugely powerful.
Until I know this, I'm a victim of the weather.
Sunny day: happy, life is good. Cloudy: miserable, struggling life, lousy relationships, nothing to offer the world, universe doesn't support me, even the dog has given up on me.
This is no way to live, believing the sun has ceased existing whenever a cloud rolls by, believing who you really are has anything to do with these fickle, up-and-down ego storms.
We are larger than our thoughts and feelings.

Drop the weeny, weather-dependent picture of yourself. It doesn't fit and it doesn't serve.

Lots of love.

Ego Deals

I want to be free as long as:
- I maintain my standard of living
- my friendships don't end
- my family doesn't suffer
- I'm still successful
- I'm still attractive
- I still fit in

Ego deals. Egos holding us hostage.
Question these.
The reason I want most of these things in the first place is my mistaken belief that they make me free.

They're fakes. I mean, they're fine, they're lovely, but they have nothing to do with real freedom.
We know this already at some level.
It is possible to choose freedom and trust what follows.

Hope this serves.
Lots of love.

Every Set Of Eyes We Meet Today

Every set of eyes we meet today is a chance to learn everything there is to know about love and fear, letting go, choosing to be open, choosing to be here and now, choosing to be really alive.
(Fully alive: the state we're hoping to reach by finding more money, the right work, the right vacation, the right lover, the right snack, the right body, the right car. Talk about confusion.)
Eyes.
The woman at the coffee drive through. The cashier at the grocery store. Your dog. The friend you think you know already. The colleague, even if he says exactly what he always says.
Stop thinking you know anybody. What you know is your repeated thoughts about them. That makes for a really boring existence.
Be reckless. Be brave. Know nothing.
Go in as student, as explorer. Go with new eyes, new ears.
Be willing to see and be seen - freshly, deeply.
#dontsleepwalkthedayaway
#everydaycanbewideopen

Hope this serves.
Love.

Fall Backwards Into the River

There is a kind of laughing, mind-blowing ecstasy in becoming aware that life happens through you - not to you, from you, because of you.
The weeny me/you thing is such a drag.
Let go, lift your arms to the sky, and fall backwards into the river.

Hope this serves.
Love.

Fear Comes And Goes

Fear comes and goes. Don't let it be the loudest voice in the room.
Shout yes.

Lots of love.

Feelings Aren't Who You Are

There's this beautiful time when we decide to feel what we feel. To be honest about our emotions and to leave denial and repression behind. It's frightening, alive, and a bit precarious.
It feels like life flowing through.
There may come another time when we feel owned by our emotions, dragged by a rope and smashed to bits behind our feelings. Blindsided by anger, sadness, resentment, despair, etc.
This doesn't feel like life flowing through. It feels like a car accident that won't stop.
Here's something to consider:
Feelings can be fabulous just like thoughts can be fabulous.
But they aren't who you are.
Like thoughts, they are collections of energy that flow through you.
Appreciating your feelings is different than holding them hostage and somehow convincing yourself that they own you.
I can't help it, we say. They're just there, and huge. They feel bigger than I am.
When this happens, you have forgotten who you are.

You are something deeper and larger than those energies passing through. Spend a bit more of your gorgeous energy investigating this.

Breathe deeply. Explore what remains when you stop touching your thoughts and feelings. Wonder about where you really begin and end. Wonder about what it is that enters a body when this body begins and what leaves a body when a body dies. That energy is enormous, connected to everything, and not tossed back and forth by feelings.

You aren't the waves on the surface of the ocean. You're the ocean.

This is more than a lovely idea. Explore it until you know it, and feelings will never own you again.

Hope this serves.
Love.

Follow Your Heart

Worrying about the opinions of others means I'm missing the point of my entire existence.
That's why they say follow your heart - your heart - not Bob's heart, your mother's heart, your kids' hearts, your hero's heart.
You are a unique point of light in the universe. Don't diminish that.

#neverhasbeenneverwillbeanotheryou

Hope this serves.
Lots of love.

For A While I Need To Stand Up For Myself

For a while, I feel the need to stand up for myself, to defend myself against horrible people and horrible circumstances. I stand my ground. I set boundaries. I fight the good fight against abusers, bullies, polluters, bad politicians, etc., etc.
It feels healthy and powerful to do this. I close the gates of my wee heart toward those who don't deserve my heart.
At some point, for some of us, this begins to feel less good, like something is happening that isn't the deepest truth. We begin to lose energy when we defend.
Until I find a better way I still feel I have to 'take care of myself' but now it leaves me drained and angry. I feel victim-y and I blame the other guy for making me feel this way. If I didn't have to defend myself against you, I'd be much happier.
Now I feel damned if I do defend and damned if I don't.
This is such an opportunity.
It's possible that we grow into a different definition of 'taking care of myself'.
It's possible, maybe, to see that there is no 'other' to defend against.
It's possible that they're doing their best just like I am.

It's possible that they act like #%€holes when threatened, just like I do.
It's possible I'm seeing them incompletely and with my own bias.
It's possible that the lousy partner or boss or kid or parent is me reflected, that the injustice and suffering I'm living is generated by my eyes, my thoughts, my history.
It's possible, even if I don't accept this reflection thing completely, to let the hostages go by letting the past go, because there is ABSOLUTELY no point in carrying that heavy trash around with you forever.
Fighting them, even with my thoughts (in the form of blame and resentment), is fighting myself, fighting love, fighting joy.
The only answer, when you get this, is to drop blame and resentment.
But I can't help it, we say.
Well, I'll bet we can for two minutes at a time, by putting my attention anywhere else.
And I'll bet we can observe that we feel way, way better when we relax the heart for the two minutes.
And I know that we can practice this.
And I know that if we do practice, it gets a bit easier.
And eventually this relaxed heart becomes easier than being pissed off.
And eventually it becomes possible to experiment with compassion for the one you've been defending against.

And eventually this becomes easier. It begins to feel good to see a beautiful, flawed human.
And eventually, loving becomes the way to end my suffering.
Eventually we choose to stop closing the gates of the heart, ever. Period.
We may get it wrong once in a while, but we know, now, that finding our way back to an open heart is the answer every single time.
Does this mean we stop advocating for better relationships, better government, a better environment, better treatment of humans everywhere? Does it mean that we let people do damage to us while we do nothing?
No.
It does mean we act from love instead of injury. We act from the greatest power.
I don't know whether we can force this transition.
Maybe we just defend until it feels too awful.
And I'm not suggesting we choose these open gates before we're ready.
You'll know when you know. And the relief will be wonderful.

Hope this serves.
Love.

For One Second

You say, I can't drop the thoughts, that's my problem. I'm good at peace in the mornings but not late in the day with my spouse and the dog and carbohydrates in my face. I can let it go except when it comes to money or oil-slicked ducks or worrying about my kids or my unimportant-but-all-consuming thighs or my crippling depression/disease/mother, etc.
It's a struggle, I tell you, and I wish I were better at it.

Stop telling this story. It's an ego job that has nothing to do with who you really are.
You don't ever need to be peaceful all day long or to permanently stop your obsessive thought loops and somehow get over what's happening in you and in the world.
This will nevah, evah be necessary.
For one second, breathe, open, let go.
Can you do that?
Yes you can.
Then you've got it. This one second is all there is.
Forget about mastering anything for all time. That's craziness.
One second, one breath, one letting go.
And now, if you're ready, drop the straitjacket stories of your struggling inadequacy.

Speak truer truths than that.
You're far more beautiful than you understand.

Lots of love.

For One Second, Right Now (which is almost identical to the last title!)

Beware of the idea that this meditation thing is hard.
I don't have the time.
I'm too tired to do it.
Piss off, my to do list is longer than War and Peace.
I'll do it when I retire.
Don't make it difficult. You don't need the full lotus, the yoga pants, the candle, the room, the monastery.
For one second, right now, make a decision to be with what is.
Bring your attention back into this room from the hoopla of the day.
If you're in the grocery store, bring your attention from that problem with your money/spouse/fatness/car into the grocery store.
Look at the people around you. Their faces. Listen to the sounds here. Smell the smells. Be here for a moment.
Then bring your attention into your body. Just notice it. (Oh, hi there! Legs! Belly! Chest! Face! Hello my honey!) Maybe enjoy the feeling of coming closer to home.
Then bring your attention to your breath. In, out. Don't make it change in any way. Just be with it for a second.

In, out. (I swoon when I get to this bit. It's like an entire universe I've been unaware of.)
Your body, breathing without any thought at all.
Air, all around you, totally available for you.
The universe breathing your body.
The universe is HAPPENING in your body.
Life happening, right here.
Life!
It's crazy. It's a MIRACLE.
Be with this breath for a moment.
This is the practice. It changes everything.

Hope this serves.
Love.

For The Longest Time

For the longest time we manage energy by creating and sustaining an identity: I'm smart, hard working, fun, lucky, charming, strong, shy, passionate, etc. My confidence comes from knowing who I am, shaping who I am, and developing a relationship between my personality and the world around me. This is self-improvement territory.

At some point there comes a desire to let all of that go and discover something open and empty through which life expresses itself.

It's like dropping your personality - your story - altogether and leaping into nothingness to find out who you really are (and who you always have been, always will be).

It's sweet, tasting this.

Lots of love your way.

Forgiveness is Health Care

I don't know whether it's possible to be truly healthy and free without learning to forgive everyone and everything.

Saying I can not forgive THAT (that parent, that spouse, that friend, that asshole, that president, that polluter, myself(!)) is like saying I am willing to sacrifice my freedom, my Essence, to spend my days building a massive wall of rocks between us on this rocky, arid island of right and wrong.

Don't choose that.

And we say, but I don't choose it! I can't help it!

This is absolutely false. We choose our thoughts all day long. With the huge judgements, we've simply repeated our thoughts so often that they feel solid and permanent.

Make a choice to dismantle these judgements, to soften them.

Remember that nothing real about you holds judgement.

Ego is the only thing that riles against forgiveness and ego is nothing more than a kid having a tantrum in a grocery store. That kid is exhausted. That kid needs a nap and someone more mature to lean on. Remember this when it feels difficult.

Your heart, your centre, KNOWS that we are all one and that Love is the answer no matter how great the challenge, no matter how 'wrong' the 'wrong'.
Give up your righteousness, your need to be right.
(Is this hard? Sometimes it is, yes. So what? Laugh at yourself and get on with it.)
Choose an open heart, inclusiveness, compassion, forgiveness.
The rest is junk. Drop it, drop it, drop it.
Start with small ones, work your way to the big ones.
Commit to it.
This is health care.

Hope this serves.
Love.

Forgiveness #2

Forgiveness never, ever has anything to do with the other guy - doesn't matter what they did, whether or not they want forgiveness, whether or not they'll ever regret their words or actions, whether or not they'll stop doing the awful thing.
It feels as though this makes it all harder (how the #% ¥£ do I forgive an ass who wants to remain an ass?, we ask), but what it really does is clarify what's happening with energy.
Until I forgive, I have slammed shut the doors of my heart. This may satisfy and protect my ego, but it is absolutely the opposite of what my heart is here for.

Your heart needs love, generosity, openness. Do not slam the doors.
As soon as you slam the doors you've cut off your own energy.
Does that mean I stand there while someone pours nasty, lousy, crabby energy my way?
It depends on how it feels.
If I'm solidly grounded and I care about this person and the junk is minor and I see that it's their pain or fatigue coming my way, and if it feels good to do this, I may just stand there and love them until something shifts.

If it feels gross and I'm ungrounded and I can't find love at the moment, I walk away. I walk far enough away that I can feel love again.
Sometimes I need to love the other person from a distance for a while before I can love them face to face again.
Sometimes this means leaving the house, leaving town, leaving the continent, leaving the marriage, etc., but it doesn't mean I have to close my heart for ever more.
So love face to face or love from a distance.
Either way, love is who we are. So closing the heart is like choking off your own spirit and opening the heart open is an act of self-love.
We make the choice.

Hope this serves.
Love.

Freedom Isn't Hard

Pointing toward home:
Freedom isn't hard.
If you find yourself thinking it's hard, or a struggle, or beyond you, be aware that this is a mind game only.
Your mind may love the struggle gig, the I-am-not-enough gig, the it-will-take-me-forever-to-get-this-who-I-really-am gig.
Nonsense. All of that is a head game. We get a bit mesmerized by the game, that's all.
If for one second, right now, you can see it as a head game, and know you are something underneath the struggle, you've found yourself.
Freedom isn't hard.
You are the freedom you sense underneath the noisy game.
Say yes to this perspective and see what happens.

Enormous love sent your way.
So grateful for this conversation.

Gorgeous People Everywhere, #1

There's a woman who works at our post office downtown.
She's tall, strong looking, blonde/grey, and has a good, big mouth and therefore a good, big smile. She's missing at least one part of one finger.
You probably know her.
At some point during each trip to the post office, it occurs to me that I hope she's working because of the way her wide open friendliness makes me feel like a human being. She's alive.
It also occurs to me as I turn the corner on Worthington each time that she once mentioned having survived a tragedy. I suspect it was her kid. I suspect there was a death. She didn't spell it out, but that was what hung in the air during one over-the-counter chat. I fell in love with her that day. It was something about the way she shared herself and her history for a moment and then moved on. How can you not love that?
During this week's visit, we laughed about what it is to live in Northern Ontario: the short summer, the relentless bugs, the different ways to combat the relentless bugs. (I moved to the country last year. The bugs are formidable. I look for tips.)

She mentioned two things which, in combination, crack me up. The first is that she stuffs Bounce sheets (things that go in a clothes dryer) under her bra straps. Mosquitoes hate them, she said. The other thing she does when the bugs are particularly bad is to wear a baseball cap and to stick a green mosquito coil on the brim and light it. Between the smoking hat and the smelly dryer sheets, she can enjoy being outdoors in the summer even if she looks like a total lunatic.
It makes me aware that you can try to be someone other than who you are and be somewhere other than where you are, both of which make you look like you're in a witness protection program, which makes you and everyone around you slightly uncomfortable and less alive.
Or you can say yes to who you are and exactly where you are in life and be singularly radiant.
That's what she is.
Go there. Meet her. Tell me what you see. Better still, tell her what you see.

Thanks for the conversation.

Grief Comes And Goes

Grief comes and goes, like a cloud passing by. Prolonged suffering happens when I hang on to grief (or fear, anger, blame, shame), when I take my thoughts to it over and over.
The feeling, which begins as a drive-by cloud, becomes my habit, my addiction. Then it becomes my identity.
Feel what you feel and let it go. It isn't who you are. You've got your poor head stuck in a cloud, that's all.

Who you are is deeper, clearer, calmer, truer, and more joyous than any weather system.
You know this.

Lots of love.

Hearts Are Designed To Be Open

You can't do a thing about anyone's opinion of you. Worrying about that is a twisted, needy use of your energy.

What you can do is keep your heart open in their direction -- not in order to change their opinion, but to take best care of both of you.

Hearts are designed to be open and we're designed to serve Love.

This is why the whole world feels like hell when we close the gates.

Hope this serves.
Love.

Here Is a Good Place

Here is a good place. Now is a good time.
I have air to breathe every single time I inhale (which feels like a miracle, when I stop to appreciate it), my heart continues to beat and send out blood and oxygen to every single cell in my body (!), my neurons continue to fire, my brain continues to interpret wavelengths in the form of smell, sound, touch, taste, and sight.
This body moves.
There's probably a bit of food in the fridge. (If not, I'll interpret a few wavelengths as hunger.)
I'm alive. LIFE moves through this body, this brain, this heart.
Why are we not more amazed by this when our eyes open in the morning?
Is there something more interesting or important on CNN or on the to-do list?
Or something more interesting or important about the bad phone call last night, the rickety friendship, the interview next week, or about my dysfunctional childhood forty years ago?
Here, now, is the only place where life is really happening.
Here, now is the point of power.
Here, now, is where the questions and answers get really simple and straightforward, where you know what

to do right now, what you can take care of and what needs to be surrendered.
It's heaven, letting go of the rest.
Being here, now is the practice.

Hope this serves.
Love.

Holding Judgements

When I hold a judgment about someone (think parents, exes, former friends, politicians with bad hair or control issues, crap bosses or business partners, lion killers, - when I hear their names and my face hardens, my thoughts harden, my words harden, my heart squeaks shut - it always, always means that I am not at home in myself. My thinking has a glitch in it. I'm off centre. I'm not awake.

And I know it because I feel like hell. (If we say, no I don't feel like hell - I hate that guy and it makes me feel excellent - we're either still in the kindergarten love program or we're lying or we're speaking about one moment of relief where we allow ourselves to feel something honest after years of muted denial. This last kind of moment is fabulous and constructive but it will not serve you to stay there.)

I've forgotten that we're all human - flawed on the surface and perfect underneath. That buffoon, no matter how (in)famous, is human. No human wakes up deciding to be an asshole. We're all doing our best to find our way home.

I've forgotten how astoundingly off course, idiotic, and unkind I've been during my own life.

I've forgotten that we're all absolutely connected. My energy affects them just as theirs affects me.

I've forgotten that the only sane thing to do when faced with conflict is to add love. Love is the only energy that warms, elevates, clarifies, dissolves, opens. Judgement is mistaken thinking. Put it down. Don't kick yourself in the head for doing it, just put it down. Would you rather be correct in judgement or be in Love?

Hope this serves.
Love.

Honour Your Voice

Yes, we want to be kind to others.
Watch that this doesn't translate to abandoning your own voice, your own instincts, your own dreams, your own sense of what is true, for the approval of others.
Big difference.
You're here to do more than make the egos around you feel safe.
Hope this serves.
Love.

How Different Would Your Life Be If

How different would your life be if you weren't afraid of looking like an idiot, weren't afraid of being killed by criticism, weren't afraid of being laughed at, weren't afraid of being dumped, weren't afraid of looking irrelevant, useless, old, fat, and completely untalented, weren't afraid of saying exactly what you feel, weren't afraid of hurting feelings, weren't afraid of wanting what you really, truly want, weren't afraid of dying alone in poverty with thirty kinds of cancer gnawing away at your unattractive body?
Just asking. (Insert the winking emoticon.)
If you can't leap right to fearlessness, maybe you can dream of being open, fantastically vulnerable, trusting, uniquely important in this universe, and ALIVE.
Devote some of your energy to this.
Don't let fear run the show.
Dream your way to courage.
This is a worthy practice.

#yourvoicematters

Hope this serves.
Love.

Hum With Love First

It's tempting to motivate yourself by pushing against the things you don't like: sexism, racism, homophobia, poverty, environmental messes, your thighs.
And for a while it will feel energetic and expansive to do the push. Being against something is better than being depressed and lifeless.
At some point you may find that the push against contracts and diminishes your energy, drawing your thoughts toward every crappy bit of news in the universe.
You begin to hum with despair, bitterness, fear, etc.
When this happens, it's useful to shift focus to what you love to see: humans honouring humans, humans honouring the planet, humans trusting what life brings, humans laughing about their own thighs.
Create gorgeous pictures to walk toward, rather than grim pictures to fight.
Read selectively, think selectively, speak with this conscious intent.
Hum with love.
Then choose your actions.
This isn't denial, it's constructive, powerful use of our energy.

Hope this serves.

Love.

I Am Large Enough To Be Here, There, And In All The Space Between

Question the idea that you are this thing that is enclosed by your skin and ends at your toes, your fingertips, your eyeballs.
Who decided that you end here? And why?
What if I extend as far as my smell extends? If that's the case, I am as big as this house, big enough to include the bacon frying downstairs this morning. I'm as big as the coffee shop I sat in yesterday.
What if I'm big enough to include everything I can hear? Then I'm big enough to include the loons outside on the lake and the chickadees doing their romancing this morning.
If we use sight, I am as large as the entire lake outside my window (the entire lake inside me!).
If I use sight and sound, I'm WITH my daughter while we Skype, I'm big enough to include my mother when she laughs on the phone. I can touch my son's fingers as we text each other.
I am large enough to be here, there, and in all the space between.
If we use taste, I am tiny, tiny this morning. I taste coffee and a bit of sleepy morning residue (which is far more pleasant than it sounds).
These are all valid.

Don't be overly seduced by one sensory system. And don't buy the limiting beliefs about yourself that you inherited.

Don't be a lemming. Question these things.

Once you let this go a bit, you can play with breath. Can I inhale the trees across the lake? Can I exhale back to them? Can I touch them from here with my breath? Not by forcing it, but by focusing, allowing.

If I can, I begin to really feel how enormous I am.

Can I inhale Nepal? Can I exhale and touch Nepal? Can I be there and here and in all the space between us? Can I add love and support in this way?

Can I use my breath to be with the difficult people in my life? Breathing into them, relaxing the junk between us? Being huge, inhaling, exhaling, embracing the whole mucky situation with compassion? Forgiving them, forgiving me, letting the whole thing dissolve?

Can I breathe into the loved ones who have passed away? Inhaling, exhaling, being large enough to really be with them?

When we move beyond the tiny, fearful definitions of self and other,

I am you and You are me.

We really, really are one.

Hope this serves.
LOVE.

I Am Not My Shirt

I am not my shirt. This one we find easy. I don't get upset when holes show up, when it gets stained, when it falls apart, because I am not my shirt.
It is a bit more challenging but just as true that I am not my beliefs, not my feelings, not my reputation, not my work, not my creativity, not my hopes, not my mind, not my body.
All of these will come and go just like my shirt.

Instead of being blindsided when these things go, pay some attention to what you are underneath it all.
What's there is subtle, but real, and more solid than the stuff we think of as solid.
A whack of suffering comes from believing I am the stuff that comes and goes.
Look to what doesn't come and go.

Lots of love.

I Get Irritated Some Mornings

I get irritated some mornings when my lovely man professes to be present with me in conversation while he's looking at car ads on his laptop in bed. I say, are you with me? And what I mean is, you're not with me, look at me while we're talking.
This cracks me up. Talk about taking someone hostage.
I'm looking for someone to be with.
The solution is for me to be with me.
Am I here? Am I here? Just keep asking until I'm here.
How am I? In my heart, I mean, not in my head. Keep asking until I can feel myself. Until I have breathed myself back into this body.
When is it? When is it? Until I'm here now. Now.
And bingo, I let the hostages go. They can be wherever they want, on their own path for the day. The lovely man can look for cars, the dog can have a nap, the world can go about its business, and I am home.
#theanswerisntoutthereitsinhere

Lots of love your way.

I'm The Tree

Breathe yourself back into yourself.
It's like we've forgotten we're the tree. We're convinced we're leaves, waving around every time a breeze goes by, freaking out when the wind changes, or when we change colours, mourning when other leaves fall, terrified of falling ourselves, developing ridiculous strategies and belief systems to feel we have some control in all of it.
All I have to do is remember I'm the tree. Breathe myself back in to the unchanging thing, to the still place.

Then I can remember that it goes even further than that. I'm Life expressing itself as the tree. Life, Peace, Home, Truth, Wholeness, Love, Universe, God, Energy. Whatever you feel best calling it. That is what we are.
Keep breathing yourself back in.

Lots of Love your way.

I'm Not Felled By Gratitude Every Day, But When I Am....

I'm not felled by gratitude every day.
Cynicism is easier. So are fear, guilt, shame, insecurity, envy.
I do understand the importance of finding my way to gratitude.
I have toenails. I have toes. I have nostrils and many other body parts. (Observe and set aside the voice that says, yeah, fat body parts, saggy body parts.)
I have children I really like and love.
The sun came up today. Such consistency! Such a beautiful thing to count on when I go to bed at night.
Gravity happens. Such consistency! So good to know my feet are on the ground.
The air smells good. The waves outside my window are miracles of frequency and matter and they sound good.
My mind is curious and useful. An excellent tool.
My heart is an excellent guide and master.
Good things happen every day.
Life is kind even when difficult things happen.
Humans are resilient. I am a resilient human.
Breakfast was good.
Coffee is beautiful.
I am alive today. There is such potential.
I love that my thoughts change everything. They really

do determine the universe I live in.

I love that I could be tied to a wheelchair in a prison cell and still have the power to change my thoughts, change my universe.

This day in front of me is wide open.

In this way, I find gratitude. I find it and grow it until, some days, I'm felled by it.

Why bother? Because gratitude is one of the great lifters, the great enlighteners.

I am not felled by gratitude every day, but when I am, I am home. I become who I really am. I remember.

Hope this serves.
Love and thanks.

If A Problem is Staring You in the Face

If a problem is staring you in the face and you don't know what to do, get quiet, stay open, and wait.
It is so tempting to flap around like a fish out out water, grasping and desperate and horribly uncomfortable. Minds, which thrive on this flapping, love this. (But I have to know today! And I have no idea what to do! What if I make the wrong decision? What if my decision commits me to a horrible future? I've done four pages of pros and cons, but I've been wrong before. What happens if I'm wrong again? Am I just being lazy or irresponsible by waiting? Etc.)

Get yourself back in the water. The first thing, always, is to remember who you are.
Be here, now, breathe, and wait quietly.
This is how the perfect answer arrives.

Hope this serves.
Lots of love.

If This Were Your One Moment

If this were your one moment of existence - this one second of this life - would you spend it thinking about your plans for the weekend, your boredom with the work in front of you, being pissed off at anyone for anything, the idea that the size of your ass or your bank account or your success or failure matters at all? Or would you weep, feeling air move across your tongue and watching your arms move, feeling your eyelids open and close, noticing we're all here in this miracle together?

Where you put your attention matters.

Hope this serves.
Love.

If We Trusted

If we trusted, we'd let go. We'd "fall back into the arms we cannot see",
and all our persistent mental churning would lose its power.
(Omg, if only I understood, if only my mortgage were paid off and my retirement income all set I could focus on this, if I could lose twenty pounds I could afford to worry about enlightenment. Hell, I've got kids and parents to worry about not to mention that knocking sound the car is making and the fact that I don't love my spouse. This list will never, never end.)

Funny, isn't it? We won't let go until we experience it, and we can't experience it until we let go.
What to do? Maybe we have to put the mental junk down - every time it shows up - and decide where our attention belongs.
What do you want most?

Hope this serves.
Love.

If You Don't Love The Story

It's so strange, the way we refer to our past as though it matters, as though what my parents or boyfriend or teacher or ex-husband did years ago is relevant.
I can keep it relevant by breathing life into it over and over. If I love the story, why not?
But if I don't love the story, if it creates suffering, then let it go.
It's as easy as exhaling.

Lots of love your way.

If You Want To Be Alive

It's so simple!
If you want to be alive, find a practice that opens your heart every day.
Do it before you leave the house. Do it over your morning coffee, or do it before you get out of bed.
Don't get caught up in making it perfect or it'll become another thing to beat yourself up about not doing.
This never needs to be perfect.
It is practice.
Open, open.
Thanks, thanks.
Bring your attention to your quiet centre. (If you can't find one, don't wrestle with this.)
Let go, let go.
Love for me, love for you.
Breathing in, breathing out.
Surrender the idea that I'm in charge.
Surrender the idea that I need to manage anyone or anything other than my own energy.
Take loving care of my own energy.
Open, open.
Thanks, thanks.
In this way, we change the world when we walk out the door. We see ourselves differently, we see others differently, we hear them more deeply, we love them more freely.

We remember who we are.

#loversasactivists

Hope this serves.
Love.

In Conflict, Do What Brings Relief

Sometimes, particularly if you've been raised to be a sweet peacekeeper, the thing to do is give yourself permission to hate the other guy's guts. You're probably justified and you have the right to feel whatever you feel. And no amount of repressing will make those feelings go away. Hate them forever if that brings you continued relief.

Once I know I have the right to my feelings and my expression, though, I may not cling to this first phase for long.

What I notice then is that the relief from shaking my fist at the other guy is very temporary. I feel worse instead of better when I hang on to crummy thoughts about them. (We choose those thoughts. Doesn't feel like it, but we do.)

I don't love the bitter hag energy that hanging onto conflict creates. It drags me down, makes me a touch less radiant.

I may decide, instead, to find a place where I can love us both, or at least move toward that.

I remind myself that we're all doing our best. I remind myself of all the times I've been an #%€hole. I remind myself that freedom and generosity feel better. I remind myself that learning to love them is learning to love me. I look for humour in the conflict.

In this way, I soften things so that they can shift more easily.

If I can then hang out with this person and see them with loving eyes, yay.

If not, I may back up, go for a walk, stop calling, I may eventually leave the work situation or the marriage, whatever it takes, to find a position of love.

(Note any resistance to letting the other person off the hook. Sometimes I'd rather be right and know they're wrong rather than open my gorgeous heart. Holy insane, right?)

Why bother looking for and finding love?

Because that lets both of the hostages go.

Find love and we're free.

Hope this serves.

Love and thanks.

It Only Takes One Sane Person

The goal is to add love to every situation.
Which of course is easy to do at weddings and around babies and runs for good causes and while being rewarded for your brilliance at work or home.
So much more challenging during conflict, failure, your non-brilliance, the other guy's boneheaded defensive moves, around deaths, shootings in Parliament, environmental disasters, scary-as-shit world events.
We have a basic human fear of things that feel bad. But there's where love matters most, and where we serve.
So go ahead, react, close up, get angry or despairing or whatever happens in the moment.
And then, as soon as you're able, get your heart legs under you. Remember what serves you and your world best.
The second you feel able to choose, choose openness, compassion, generosity, forgiveness, community.
With time, we begin to choose this sooner and sooner, knowing that this choice is the answer.
It only takes one sane person to change the room.

Hope this serves.
Love.

It's Love or Fear, Honey

"Move, but don't move the way fear makes you move."
Rumi

This makes me laugh. I have to add: be willing to tell the truth about what is making you move.
(I've made a lot of murky moves in my life by convincing myself they were not fear-based. I was too afraid to tell the truth about being afraid. A sitcom of insecurity.)
Every decision is about love or fear.
Remember who you are. Then choose.

Hope this serves.
Love.

It's Not About Becoming Somebody

"The game is not about becoming somebody. It's about becoming nobody." Ram Dass

Oh, there is such pleasure in this: letting life happen through me instead of making something of myself, defending that self, worrying about that self, feeling guilty about what that self did yesterday, making decisions for that self, comparing that self to every other self.
Imagine the freedom in dropping this!
#we'lldancethehappiestdance

Lots of love.

Joyous, Generous, Quiet, Alive

We devote so much energy to creating an identity that is more successful than, safer than, smarter than, more attractive than, more interesting than, more wanted than, more valuable than, more driven or ambitious than, more accomplished than....
Than what? What would we be if we stopped building this?
Lazy? Poor? Lonely? Depressed? Worthless? A wasted life? Ignored? Unseen? Unhealthy? Off the radar of the happening world? Unimportant?
Which of these is it for you? Or is it something else?

Maybe all of that is true.
At least maybe that's what the mind would register initially.
With continued letting go, it may look different. Empty, relaxed, full, complete, open, roomy, joyous, generous, quiet, alive.
Do you know this already?

Hope this serves.
Love.

Lean Toward Love and Watch What Happens

People say, you're not looking objectively at the world. You've just decided to see it as beautiful and love-filled - even the conflicted relationships, the opinions of others, the inner stormy gunk, the lion killers, the twists and turns of the day.
And I say yes. That's exactly right.
My thoughts determine what I see and how I see.
And I have absolute choice in my thinking.
(The first thought that swings by may be judgemental or fearful or otherwise less than open and generous, but we choose to carry that thought or drop it. We choose to follow crap thoughts down a path or to leave them and walk down a lighter path. Choice, choice, choice.)
Why does this matter?
Because I am a more useful human being when I am open minded, open hearted, lighthearted, and disentangled.
Lean toward love and watch what happens.

Hope this serves.
Love.

Let It All Unfold

Just let it unfold.
This sounds like the punchline to a bad laundry joke, but there's a lot of peace in it when I'm willing to listen.

Lots of love.

Let People Be Whole and New

Another reason to breathe yourself open this morning is that people are not who you think they are.

We have these captions that go with the people in our lives:

he's untrustworthy, she's flaky, he's the smart one, he is always late, she's an entertainer, she is so superficial, he's arrogant, she's confident but she's a bully, she's an alcoholic, he can't get his act together.

We hang onto these impressions for decades, don't we?

We have a hundred reasons for doing this. If you have bullied me twenty times, I protect myself the next time by labelling you a bully. I keep my distance even when your hand is touching me. I will not be blindsided by you again. I will not be hurt by you or let down.

I close my heart next time your name comes up. I feel safer and smarter in the world, but now I'm someone with a closed heart.

Who loses here?

And what happens when I make those judgements about myself? (Can I be the kind of person who creates captions about you without also making them about myself?)

I'm not creative. I'm lousy with money. I'm terrible with conflict. It's too late for me to do what I really

want. I'm arthritic. I'm not the sharpest tool in the shed.
None of these are accurate. Even if they were accurate before (and most of them were at best slivers of accuracy, they never described a whole being!), we have NO IDEA what's true now unless we enter NOW nakedly, without captions.
Forget about the safety of definitions.
Nothing that closes your heart is safe.
Let people be whole and new in your eyes. What a gift.
Let you be whole and new in your eyes. What a gift.
And so much closer to truth.

Hope this serves.
Love.

Letting The Hostages Go

Sometimes we get caught thinking we know how things should be for us and for other people.
That guy should support my projects more because I support his. It's only fair.
That guy never returns my emails. He should be more polite, more responsible.
My dad should eat better to help slow the progression of his dementia.
My dad's wife should do something about that.
My great friend who lives across the country should call more often if she cares about friendship.
I should do more to take care of my friendships so that I don't end up living above a Mike's Mart, eating dry cat food, drinking chocolate milk, and smoking cigarettes in solitude for the last years of my life.
I should have breastfed my kid longer. (That kid is in his late twenties now, but this one still goes through my head.)
My lovely man should compliment me more often, touch me more often (without going straight for the genitalia), share his feelings more often, understand my feelings without me having to spell them out, improve his grammar, assume I'm right in all disputes, and clip the dog's talons more frequently. (Spouses get the worst of us, don't they?)

Etc.

Today I will practice letting the hostages go.

When one of these 'should' thoughts appears, I'll drop it. Let it float by. Not feed that one today.

I will walk my path and allow you to walk yours.

In this way, we find some space, some openness. And we allow ourselves to be here.

#feelslikefreedom
#thisiswherelifeis

Hope this serves.
Love.

Love And Let Go of Every Single Thing

Some days the world is so generous and good, so filled with beautiful people, that I can hardly stand up. You know how it is, when you're afraid to go for groceries knowing you'll weep your ugliest weep when the cashier smiles. Today is one of those days for me.
And this, in the middle of all the sadness and cruelty in the same world.
How can we live with this mix without being wrecked? I can only do it by being completely present (which makes me feel huge enough to contain it all) and by doing my best to love and then let go of every single thing.

#likelearningtofly

Hope this serves.
Love.

Loving Each Other As Hard as We Can

What a week.
A nephew of mine died in his sleep at 27.
And I've been with my dad all week after one of his frequent close calls with death. He's 86 and has dwindled over the last few years.
We chat and his once formidable mind comes and goes. It is extremely beautiful as long as I allow myself to be fully with him as he is right now. It's like seeing him for the very first time in some ways.
I've been looking into long term care for him. It's a confusing mess of stress, red tape, and inadequate resources.
While visiting one nursing home yesterday I passed an old woman in a wheel chair who was cradling a baby doll against her chest. The woman's face was radiant. She couldn't talk but she beamed at us as though she was on fire inside. A happy new mother.
I dunno. It broke my heart wide open. We SO have no idea where this life is going and what it's going to look like at each stage and how long it's going to last.
It makes me think that the only sane response to such uncertainty is to love each other as hard as we can, to forgive everything, to be grateful for this second in time, and to drop everything else.

Glad to be here with you.

Love.

Low Level Suffering

There's a kind of low level, habitual suffering that adds up to chronic, dull, dense energy.
First thing in the morning:
A little more sleep would have been nice.
Coffee. Where's the coffee.
Man, the snow is deep out there.
Yikes, I can still feel that lower back.
Wish that project funding would show up today.
So-and-so is ruining the environment.
Wish I weren't so lazy.
etc.
It's a list of minor judgements and complaints. Objections to what is.
It adds up to a foggy, resistant energy, 100% of it generated by our minds, not by actual circumstances.
It's just ego doing it's crabby thing.
I doubt that mind/ego ever stops this.
But we have choice.
I can see this fog for what it is and snap out of it.
It's possible to see those thoughts and not own them or be owned by them this morning.
It's possible to focus instead on the miracle of breathing in and out.
I mean, really, if you were witnessing your breathing for the first time, would you not be amazed by it?

Who's doing this thing, this contraction and expansion that allows me to be alive at all this morning? When I let it all be new, which only requires that I be here and now, I look across the bed and think, o my god, there's another human BEING in this bed! There's a doggo BEING lying across my LEG! And I have EYEBALLS to see this with! And oh my god, YOU have EYEBALLS that see it all COMPLETELY DIFFERENTLY.
And there's a WORLD outside the window! A WORLD! Look at SNOW! Are you telling me that those SNOWFLAKES outside are unique? And that they're there because of how this PLANET is moving around this SUN!?
What the hell! Why are we not all freaking out about this?
(What a massive, cosmic joke, that all of this is going on while we complain about having to shop for tonight's dinner.)
All this miraculous stuff going on in every moment. Two minutes of being here, now, and I laugh at myself for ever complaining.
The fog lifts and I remember.

#complainingisadrag

#youaremorebeautifulthanthat

Hope this serves.

Love.

Luckily, This is Not Rocket Science

Luckily, this is not rocket science. (I feel for rocket scientists and brain surgeons. We're always referencing them when it comes to difficult intellectual tasks. They must feel horrid pressure to be smart 24/7. And I'll bet they're idiots, sometimes, just like the rest of us.)
I wake up, I notice how I feel.
If my first few thoughts are, wow, it's another arctic day in this perpetual winter, my head feels a bit thick, I'm not sure I'm up to today's writing/skiing/driving, socializing, etc., I stop.
This complaining 'bleh' state is one of my hellish default vibes but it doesn't feel very alive and it isn't who I really am.
(It is often the vibe of media and of casual conversation, which is one of the reasons you have to become responsible for it yourself if you want something different.)
I make a choice to change it, to see through it to something more true.
I do that by contemplating who I really am underneath the layers of thought.
Or by dropping all thoughts and focussing on breath.
Or by spending time with the three million things I'm thankful for in my life.

Or by rubbing my dog's belly and watching her accept love without reservation. She's a love pig.
Or by creating a sitcom from my repetitive 'bleh' thoughts, which are sadly unoriginal and mostly insane. Find a sense of humour, you ridiculous squirrel.
I do this until it works. Until I feel myself open.

We have choice. Making the choice to become lighter and freer is the practice.
There is no pass or fail, here. If you practice for two minutes, you're in a better place. If you practice all day long, you're flying.
As always, this is me talking to me (singular, collective, I have no idea), and is nevah, evah intended as advice.

Hope it serves.
Much love your way.

Lurching Ciabatta

"Don't drink at the water's edge. Throw yourself in. Only then will your thirst be quenched." Jeanette Berson

I used to think I would instantly and effortlessly dissolve into love by embracing these statements, that they would be a kind of miracle cure for my humanness. I hoped for that. Fervently.
I also hoped that dissolving into love would be a pretty process, that letting go of junk would be graceful and lovely. (Think Audrey Hepburn.)
But every day I wake up and am still human. Every day the letting go is a decision. And sometimes the process is ugly and obscenely repetitive.
The 'throw yourself in' quotes are still gorgeous. They make me feel courageous and stir up a central, powerful longing for freedom, a kind of recognition of oneness.
They do send me running toward the water, but they also make me laugh, now, because of the human crust that I start out with every single day.
Now I know, I trust, that I am water. I am a drop in the great ocean. In the big picture, I am the great ocean.
But some days it doesn't feel like this.

Some days I feel like a huge, thirsty ciabatta bun lurching on doughy legs toward the deep end of the pool. A crusty, chewy, aromatic, not particularly healthy, completely manufactured being hits the water and becomes a soggy, gross, disgusting, broken down mess. It discovers itself to be flour and air and not much else. It accepts this and decides for the four billionth time to go. It floats until waterlogged and then sinks with a bit of kicking and screaming into the constant, deep end of love.

The point of this lousy analogy is just to say that some days this trip is peaceful and easy. Some days it isn't.Be gentle with yourself for being human.
Even when it's messy, we know that love is where we come from and is where we're headed.
Be brave. Keep jumping.

Hope this serves.
Love.

Make Gratitude Your Practice

Make gratitude your practice.
I read this and shake my head at how cliche it sounds.
Yeah, yeah, yeah.
Thanks for my life, blah, blah.
Thanks for all the stuff I have, blah, blah.
This is supposed to be good for me, blah, blah.
If I could wave a magic wand, I would take us all to a place, a state, in which we practice thanks every morning - on paper (for me), in our hearts, out loud - until we're felled by this MOMENT we're living. Felled by the aliveness of it.
So blown by it that we become aware of the miracle it is to exchange eye contact today, words today, feelings today.
Why don't we take it this far and see what happens.

Hope this serves.
Love.

Moments of Crazy Love

There's this feeling that washes over sometimes when I'm surrounded by strangers. It happened in COSTCO last week, and again on Sunday in a Starbucks. Then again last night at my band practice.
I play flute in a beginner's band. We're not great yet. Just to give you a clearer picture of how not great we are, one of the featured pieces for our upcoming concert (our first one!) is the B flat scale.
And we're nervous about getting it right in public. Yesterday we were playing a kindergarten version of Ode To Joy, straight quarter notes and half notes - nothing tricky, a bit plodding.
And out of nowhere my eyes started weeping, my nose got drippy, and I was overcome with a sort of devastating joy at being in a roomful of HUMANS, together on this planet, living lives in various bodies and minds, but totally, totally, TOGETHER in this. Not together in the music (we are SO not together in the music - the saxes often finish bars ahead of the rest of us and I still struggle to hit half the notes I'm aiming for), but together in ALL OF THIS.
The blast of feeling knocks me over. All of a sudden I really see faces and eyes. Everyone is beautiful.
A roomful of people reading music (or drinking cappuccinos or buying monster packs of toilet paper), all

perfectly coordinated at some deeper level of Ode To Joy, breathing into each other, touching the earth one foot at a time, thinking, feeling, being.

My guess is that this is a glimpse of the truth that exists underneath everything.

Another guess is that the practice of being here, now, opens the door to this experience.

Hope this serves.
Love.

Morning Practice - Imagine The World We Create By Doing This Together

A morning practice that breathes me back into myself changes everything.

It changes every decision from whether or not to have another coffee, which projects I'll work on today, whether or not yesterday's parking ticket makes me angry with myself and the parking ticket guy, whether or not I'm afraid and controlling about my future, whether or not I worry about my kids, whether or not I love the lovely man beside me in bed - you know, just to name the first of four thousand examples that come to mind.

When I take the time to come back to right here and right now (before my mind carries me too far away from sanity), my decisions are made from the centre and not from the ragged, needy edges.

My choices become a bit clearer and feel simpler. And always there is a sense that everything is okay. The world is lighter.

I do this for myself. For the reduction of suffering. For the good vibes. But there's no question that everyone from the parking ticket guy to my kids to my lovely man benefit from my practice. They all become loves instead of targets.

Do I veer away from this during the day?
Sure.

But it's wayyyyyy easier to come back with a breath or two if I started the day with an open, knowing heart. Imagine the world we create by doing this together.

Hope this serves.
Love.

My Dad, Revisited

Many thanks for all your gorgeous thoughts about my dad.
His new drugs had him seeing marching bands and silver-clad angels in the driveway yesterday. Not what we'd hoped for.
I want to say something more about it, just to offer one perspective.
I don't resent this dementia at all. I don't feel it's taken him away.
Yes, it's frightening sometimes, and frustrating.
He's scared by it and ashamed some days. I think his wife is terrified, angry, lonely, and a hundred other understandable things.
We're all learning or trying to learn how to surf a huge, unfamiliar wave. For me, the surfing has something to do with learning to be broken hearted and openhearted at the same time. To not distance myself from it.
Basic life lessons, love lessons.
It is what is. His mind is breaking down the way cardiovascular systems and musculoskeletal systems break down, eventually.
He and I talk about this being the part of his body that's wearing out. He knows now that this'll probably be the way it goes for him, rather than cancer or a heart attack. He's going the wonky head route.

I ask him whether it's okay that there are marching bands in the driveway or strangers in the room that the rest of us can't see. He doesn't like it happening, but they are his reality some days. And who's to say his reality is any less valid than ours? Maybe the angels are there and we're the ones who can't see.
I like going with him into these visions. I like being with him rather than fighting it.
People say dementia takes loved ones away.
I feel the opposite. I see a frailer version of my dad, but it's like meeting him as a kid, or maybe just an adult with an undefended heart and mind. He's gorgeous. In this way I feel as though dementia has offered me a clearer view of him. I'm grateful to have this while he's here.
I'm also amazed, amazed, when I read your warm words to realize again that we're all in this together. There's nobody out there who hasn't been through this or something similar (or something harder) with a parent, a kid, a spouse, a great friend. You can't throw a rock without hitting someone who is learning to surf a new wave.
What an excellent thing to contemplate when I meet the next pair of eyeballs today.

Hope this serves.
Love and thanks.

My Teacher's Better Than Your Teacher

The thing that cracks me up this morning:
Over the years, I've had so many great teachers.
It seems there's been an endless line of them going back forever. (I remember reading early Wayne Dyer and Maya Angelou in my parents' library when I was eight or nine and thinking, something IMPORTANT is going on here. Wake UP!)
My ego does a funny thing with teachers. While I'm enamoured with one, that one is the BEST, so much wiser and closer to the truth than the others. And, if I tell the humiliating truth, my spirituality feels more evolved than the spirituality of someone who loves one of the lesser, superficial, shallow teachers.
Years go by and now my former super duper teacher looks limited, superficial, and shallow compared to the one who is my current inspiration.
My ego still wants to do this: it compares, judges, ranks.
I don't buy it quite as fully as I used to. Hard to swallow the kool-aid so completely when I've been through the cycle so many times.
And this cycle only deals with the teachers I've been able to see and learn from.
What of the teachers in disguise who are everywhere and unseen by my ego eyes???

Maybe every moment is the miraculous teacher. Really. Maybe the sound of that bird is the Dalai Lama and the smell of my coffee is Thich Nhat Hanh. The ominous sound my car is making is Pema Chödrön.
Maybe it's more like a million windows into the Great House. Slightly different, beautiful views of the beautiful centre, the Beautiful All.
Thanks for all of it, for the wonder of being a part of Something that keeps unfolding, something that is new again and new again and new again.
Who needs more than this?

Hope this serves.
Love.

Not Owned By The Parade

It feels gorgeous to detach from compulsive thinking, to let thoughts and feelings go by in a parade. I can wave at them, enjoy some clowns and not others, but I don't have to be in that parade 24/7. I am not owned by the parade, not employed by it, and under no moral obligation to analyze it in therapy for the rest of my life. The parade is not who I am.
A few steps back, the world is quiet, open, and true. I begin to see who I am beyond thought.
It's heaven.

Lots of love your way.

On Being Brave

Be brave. Practice courage in small ways so that you'll be brave enough for the big challenges.
Be a little more honest than is comfortable.
Hold eye contact for a little longer.
See yourself more honestly than is comfortable.
Stay with your gross feelings instead of running.
Be more generous with your time, your energy, your money. This takes courage.
Stay more open in the face of stuff that makes you want to close up shop: the judgement of others, whatever scares you.
Instead of jumping into conversation with your history and your opinions, keep listening.
Listen deeply, with your whole body. Allow what you hear to change you.
Question your control freak leanings. Have they really brought you joy?
It might be impossible to be both safe and free.
Open, let go.
A worthy practice over coffee on a Saturday morning.

Hope this serves.
Love.

On Being Yourself

Being yourself takes so much courage, doesn't it? It means putting yourself out there loud and proud, sometimes wrong and strong (to quote Neil, fearless leader of the Joy Band I play with), and wide open to criticism.
It means being different from the lemming standard designed to keep you safe, popular, unthreatening, and UNORIGINAL.
Accepting the lemming standard means dying at some level, because ORIGINAL is what you are.
You are a singular spark in the universe.
How absurd to hide that. How absurd to pretend to be something less than that.
Accept the fact that your being here matters.
Call it your spark, your singular set of gifts and inclinations, your divinity, your point in space and time that meets the energy of the WHOLE of the universe.
Call it whatever feels truest and wakes you up.
Decide to accept that.
And then honour it.
Act on it.
Make this your practice.
Do this today and watch what happens.

Hope this serves.
Love.

On Divinity

I want to say something about divinity. Maybe we can define that word first.

First definition:

The nature of a god. This one rubs a lot of us the wrong way because of our histories (the whole bizarre business of eight-year-olds being taught about original sin and hell, hiding in my closet to avoid wearing a doily on my head to go to chapel at boarding school to name a couple of personal ones), weird, patriarchal moralism, shunning people who leave their religions, the insanity attached to who can marry whom, and the 'god is on our side' approach to invading other countries, just to name a few examples.

Second definition:

a fluffy, creamy candy made with stiffly beaten egg whites.

Use this if it serves. It does sound divine.

Third definition:

The essence of Love on a universal scale.

The essence of Beauty, of Truth, of Harmony.

The essence of Yes, of Open, of Life Pouring Through.

The essence of Generosity and Abundance.

The essence of Connectedness.

(This one is my working definition.)

All of this is to set up the following practice for today. Two steps, both of them huge.

1. Using the definition that serves you best, Remember your divinity. Contemplate it.
You are a product of Love and you are Love's ambassador right here and right now. You are what Love is doing on this planet right now.
This matters.
2. Honour this. Act on it. Appreciate it.
Honouring it means:
Be open when it takes guts to be open.
Accept compliments. Somebody is recognizing your Beauty, your Talent, your Clarity. Say yes to that.
Treat yourself beautifully in thought, word, and deed.
Don't settle for crappy thoughts and default feelings. Catch yourself when you fall into junky thinking and re-aim.
Make eye contact. Be willing to see divinity and be seen as divinity. This can be hard, especially with people you judge as shmucks and people who scare you. Be persistent. Judgements fall away with real eye contact.
Be Generous and Forgiving. Let the people around you screw up. Don't close your heart when that happens.
Let yourself screw up. Don't close your heart when that happens.

Remember your divinity and honour it. So much more than an idea on a shelf.
This is an active, courageous practice.

Hope this serves.
Love.

On Surrendering

We're afraid that surrendering - letting go of the shore, moving into the current - means leaving the career, leaving the lover, leaving the dog, living under a bridge like a troll and learning to catch fish with my bare hands while scratching at the bugs living in my matted facial hair.
This doesn't happen very often.
The transformation is internal. It changes your heart, your eyes, your energy, your interactions. It changes this moment.
You become aware that this moment is it, it's all there is, and you've been blowing by it all your life.
The worries about the dismantled life are the ego's way of preventing the surrender and internal transformation.
The ego prefers us to judge and compete and compare and consume, and to stay really, really safe. These are lifeblood for ego.
Don't be held hostage by your ego. It'd be such a drag to live out your days ruled by such a weenie sliver of your full-hearted self.
Make a decision to stay open. (The Untethered Soul is a beautiful book for this.)
Hold eye contact. Stay open with the people who piss you off. (Think family, think people who insist on dis-

liking you every day, think exes, think old, dead friendships, think people in power who scare you.) Don't slam your heart shut with people you've decided are wrong, arrogant, unkind, or stupid. These judgements are squeezing the life out of our own hearts. It makes us dry, crispy, cynical, and deadly boring.
Say yes. Be vulnerable. Stop thinking you know the answers already.
Say yes to some bigger intelligence without having to know what that is.
Say a big fat yes to every thought and feeling that arrives and then let them all go.
This is surrender.
You can feel the current moving through you by doing this even while you're in your cubicle or greeting shoppers at the front door of Walmart.
Make this your practice.
Will you end up under a bridge? I doubt it.
Most of us will become radiant citizens in the regular (now transformed) world.
(But who cares, WHO CARES about being a troll if you're free? We'd be the richest, happiest, healthiest trolls you ever imagined.)

Hope this serves.
Love.

One Breath at a Time

The challenge is to practice staying here and now in a way that feels nurturing and encouraging rather than it feeling like a bull fight in a hurricane.
One way to do this is delight in every moment you're here.
Another is to stop beating yourself up over the moments you are distracted or carried away by thought or emotion. Tormented self-flagellation, as attractive as it is sometimes, is not the point.
An exercise:
Be immersed in making your coffee while making your coffee. Let it be a full, complete experience.
Leave your to-do list out of it for now.
Forget multi-tasking for a moment.
This is enough practice to last thirty years.
And if your life crashes to the ground at some point during those thirty years, you'll look for and find a deeper practice.
(The joke is that while making coffee, we're planning the thing we're doing at ten. And at ten, we're thinking about how this meeting is killa boring and we'd rather be at lunch and at lunch we're wishing we didn't have to go back to work but we have to to meet the payments on the hummer, and back at work we're exhausted and then we go home and try not to think

about the day. We have a few drinks and try desperately to let go for one second. HA! What a crazy sitcom! No wonder we're looking for something a little saner.)
One breath at a time. xo.

Hope this serves.
Love.

One Of The Great Cosmic Jokes

One of the great cosmic jokes:
We avoid being here, now, as though it's Ebola.
We shop, we eat, we drink, we organize, we plan, we fix, we worry, we work, we self-improve, we improve others, we take action, we stay busy, we move ahead, we talk, talk, talk, we fill our days with doing.
Why?
1. Because something about here, now is uncomfortable and scary. We are absolutely conditioned to believe that whatever is good in my life is good because of my striving. Stillness feels bad. And
2. Because we want joy. We're looking for joy. (Call this by any synonym: satisfaction, relief, accomplishment, belonging, purpose, esteem, respect, worthiness.)
There's this feeling that we've got to do something to get to the joy. Gotta change something or someone, gotta prove, gotta push, gotta get myself going, gotta find the next answer. (Gotta drive the universe.)
After a while (possibly many decades), you see this for the ego game it is.
Stop for a second.
For one moment, trust. Experiment. Be curious.
Be here fully. Right now. Sink into it. Sink further.
(Let the universe and life and your life carry on beautifully without your striving.)

Sink until you know that your thoughts are not who you are. They may be noisy guests, but you feel/know that they are not YOU.
Allow yourself to be here.
And what happens?
The seeking dissolves.
Here is what we're looking for the whole time.
This is it, this is it, this is it.
Does this mean never working or shopping or walking again?
No!
But instead of working to find joy, we now work with joy, in joy.
Gorgeous difference.

Hope this serves.
Love.

One Thought at a Time

What if every thought you have about your own deficiencies, defects, or brokenness is arbitrary and mistaken?
Maybe any unhappiness has more to do with your thinking than anything else.
This is good news because you choose your thoughts.
Beware the seductiveness of assuming your thoughts are stronger than you are, that you can't help thinking the destructive thoughts.
It's possible the first negative thought can sneak in, but as soon as you register that one, you have a choice.
I can stay with that lousy thought and pick at it like a festering scab and add to it until I'm as depressed as hell, or angry or ashamed of my own existence, or I can decide to take my mind elsewhere.
One thought at a time is all it takes.
Think about something else, stop thinking altogether, watch sitcoms, offer help to someone who needs it (offer to help someone who doesn't need it - who cares as long as it's an improvement), get outside for some air and sun, hang out with the dog.
When the lousy thoughts return, make a practice of saying no thanks.
This is a skill. Master it.
Everything is practice.

We're either practicing being victims of crappola thoughts or we're practicing thinking of ourselves as the gorgeous, well intentioned, huge hearted spirits we are.

Hope this serves.
Love.

Open

When in doubt, open.
When angry, open.
When grief stricken, open.
When ashamed, open.
When terrified, open.
When helpless, open.
When hopeless, open.
When succeeding or failing, open.
When right or wrong, open.
When dying, open.
When hurt, open.
When human, open.
When fully alive, open again.

Hope this serves.
Enormous love.

Open Feels Better Than Closed

We know that open feels better than closed.
I create openness in my body by relaxing my hands, my feet, my belly, my throat, my jaws, my tongue, my eyes, my breath, and through any kind of joyous exercise.
I create openness in my mind by saying yes to what I want instead of no to what I don't want. No (fear, judgement, worry, anger) shuts me down. Yes opens me up.
I create openness in my heart through love, thanks and forgiveness.
Some days it makes us crazy to be told these things because we're miles from authentic gratitude, for example, when it's -38 degrees outside and our ass is still too fat for our liking.
This is excellent, this knowing where we're at and not faking it.
On these days, I can still relax my hands and my feet. I can open by finding a sense of humour about my ingratitude or my fear. I can hope that real forgiveness might happen tomorrow or thirty years from now.
We don't have to get it all right today. There's no prize for being the fastest Buddha.
Just pick one form of openness that resonates today, and make it your practice.

Open is who we really are. That's why every tiny step in the direction of openness feels like heaven.

Hope this serves.
Enormous love your way.

Peace Inside, First

Peace inside, first.
Otherwise, at least superficially, you're a broken thing trying to fix a broken thing.
(And when you slow down enough, when you breathe yourself back to the sanity of this moment, you see that nothing is broken.)
So if the world looks nuts, come back.
If you're afraid, come back to now.
If you're out of whack and suffering with yourself, your lovers, friends, or enemies, come back to now.
This is not a recipe for inaction.
It's a recipe for effective change.

Hope this serves.
Love.

Practice Courage

Be brave. Practice courage in small ways so that you'll be brave enough for the big challenges.
Be a little more honest than is comfortable.
Hold eye contact for a little longer.
See yourself more honestly than is comfortable.
Stay with your gross feelings instead of running.
Be more generous with your time, your energy, your money. This takes courage.
Stay more open in the face of stuff that makes you want to close up shop: the judgement of others, whatever scares you.
Instead of jumping into conversation with your history and your opinions, keep listening.
Listen deeply, with your whole body. Allow what you hear to change you.
Question your control freak leanings. Have they really brought you joy?
It might be impossible to be both safe and free.
Open, let go.
A worthy practice over coffee on a Saturday morning.

Hope this serves.
Love.

Practices for Waking Up

One story:
A certain kind of joy, power, and freedom comes from building your identity. You create a 'you' that interacts with the world in a way that feels good. This identity has an effect and a sense of control. It has boundaries, goals, successes, failures, a defined personality, heaps of decisions about rights and wrongs, wins and losses. At some point, something about this constructed life loses its joy, maybe because it fails (illnesses that shouldn't happen, businesses that lose, relationships that crash or go on but don't satisfy) or because it wins (the good marriage, kids, career, money, health) but somehow still feels like not enough, not it, not home.
Your vision of how this should all unfold gets smacked.
And you find some hunger for ... what? For truth, for freedom, and this hunger grows and is unaddressed by your best efforts at creating a life.
Often we respond by building a new identity.
Stronger, smarter, better aimed, more ambitious, thicker skinned. Iron Man 1, 2, 3, 4, 5, etc. New career, new relationships. Re-aim, re-aim, re-aim.
At some point, if we're lucky, these reinventions will not satisfy.
We'll see them for the constructions they are.

You'll know you're here if you experience a longing for the truth that you can't shake. A kind of homesickness. (If you don't feel that longing, just go on enjoying your Iron Man 7. Really. Stop reading this.)

If you have the longing, ask yourself this:

How can an invented identity, even a 'successful' one, ever be as present, spontaneous, fresh, whole, or beautiful as who you really are underneath all of that? The thoughts, words, and actions of these identities can never be as free and true as the whole of you in the fullness of this moment.

We say, but what the hell, I have no idea who I am under all of this constructed self. I sense that I'm something more expansive, but I have no idea how to get there.

Well, the truth is you already and always exist as something whole, connected, enormous, and loving. That is who you are. That is here and now.

So if you suspect you aren't 'there', your constructed head is talking.

If you'd like to wake up from the constructed head dream, you can.

Practices.

1. **Tell the truth**. Everywhere and with everyone. To the best of your ability, stop telling canned stories - They're dead. Stop leading with your old stories, especially the ones that you've told a hundred times. You're just reinforcing an old identity. Stop trying to be anything. Just be here and tell the truth.

2. **See the truth in the other guy**. If you're seeing anything but love and light and drop-dead gorgeousness, your identities are running the show. You don't have to cure this. Just be aware.

3. **Slow down**. Most of what comes out of our mouths is lunatic chatter that has nothing to do with who we are. It is an automatic sound track. Stop. Wait. Let your words come from You. Through You.

4. Whenever you feel yourself grabbing an identity, telling an old, dead story, wishing you were more successful, in control, popular, etc., **practice instant forgiveness**. You feed your ego by beating yourself up for getting anything 'wrong'. It's a fool's game.

5. **Breathe**. Pay attention to your breath. It brings you home.

Again and always, none of this is advice. If it doesn't serve, let it run off you like water off a duck's back. If it does serve, I'm glad we're in the conversation together.

Love.

Princess Margaret Again

We've been at Princess Margaret this week. it's an enormous cancer hospital in Toronto.
If you ever want to experience the importance of loving eye contact and an open heart in the presence of fear and difficult stories, try hanging out in one of these places. (Many, many of you have, I know.)
It'll cure you of all the stupid worries we cling to about losing weight, Christmas shopping, our income, difficult family crap, whether or not we're in the right relationships. Blah, blah, blah.
Yesterday, I stood beside an older man while he pushed his wheelchair across the fifteen feet between the blood lab and an ATM on the first floor.
He was in what looked like a severe stage of Parkinson's, but it may for all I know have been a post-chemo/radiation thing, and the guy could not move except for these tiny shuffles after minutes of shaky deliberation. He had no one with him (this blows my mind, still) in this crowd of terrified first timers and possibly less terrified vets.
I asked if I could help and couldn't understand a garbled word he said in reply. He saw that I couldn't understand.
If I'd had my regular human defences up, I'd have gone back to my seat, intimidated by our failure to communicate.

Instead, this one time, I stayed with him for the eternity it took to cross the hallway. Man, it was uncomfortable. I don't know whether he even wanted me there.

I also don't know where he was going after the ATM, or whether he got there safely.

My lovely man and I went on to the wonky eye department on the eighteenth floor, which is filled with its own stories.

Afterward, with that weird mix of adrenaline, half relief, and fatigue that many of you are familiar with, I'm sure, we walked back to our hotel, giving quarters and loonies out to the sweet hearts living on the street.

Jesus. We absolutely cannot know how to create a safe life.

But we can decide to stay open to the life that presents itself. We can do our best to offer love, silently or loudly, by being still or offering touch - whatever seems honest and true at the time.

This is what I most want to be and to receive and to carry with me through this season.

Love this morning to the shaky man. I hope you made it home safely.

And love to all of you.

Hope this serves.
Love again.

Pull Yourself Out of Your Suffering

Perspective is a great thing.

Pull your nose out of your suffering as soon as you can, as soon as you'd prefer not to keep suffering. Back up until the suffering is over there somewhere, and smaller, and temporary, like a little whirling dervish of sadness or anger or bitterness or envy. It's loud when you're close to it, and gets quieter as you step back.
See it whirling underneath a huge tree in the most beautiful field, under a blue sky, with all your favourite music playing in the background. Poor wee dervish, so caught in its own spinning that it can't hear the music.
Back up until you feel a bit of compassion for the suffering.
Back up more, until the swearing, bawling, snot-nosed dervish looks funny in your gorgeous field. It's like something from a Bugs Bunny cartoon.
Back up again until it looks like a beautiful part of a beautiful whole. Until it looks like a tiny blue blur in a painting that would be missing something without some blue.

Then choose your vantage point. Would you rather be swallowed by it again, or can you see it as a small part of your rich, deep life?
This is not a way to avoid feeling. It is a way to let yesterday's suffering go so that I don't paint my entire life blue today.

Hope this serves.
Love.

Question Your Unhappiness

Question your unhappiness instead of defending it. Poke holes in it, look for alternatives, shift your attention to something gorgeous, be willing to drop it for a nanosecond.
Do you want to stay miserable just because it's justified misery?

Hope this serves.
Lots of love.

Re: Criticism

Re: fearing criticism from others.
I mean really. Can anyone else ever say anything worse than the awful stuff you say to yourself during those low moments when you MOST need loving? Take care of the critic who's doing the biggest damage. Focus your energy where it matters. Where you can change something.
Learn to speak with love and acceptance when you look in the mirror. Do this consistently, persistently, and the criticism from others will become far less important. It may sting a bit, still, but it won't kill you. (Their criticism only has power if you agree with it. And their criticism always, always has more to do with them and their needs and fears than it has to do with you.)
#bebwave

Hope this serves.
Love.

Resolutions

Historically, my big end-of-year resolutions have come from pockets of chronic dissatisfaction: I don't like this about myself, I hereby commit to being significantly different this year so that I might find it easier to like myself.
Unsurprisingly, this failed to work every single year (unless your definition of success includes finding yourself unchanged except for unprecedented levels of depression by mid-January).
The only serious commitment I make now is to practice being here, now, and open.
It's a pretty full time occupation, it feels constructive, it's gentler than the old fix-it resolutions, and everything else - my career, my body, my relationships - seems to take care of itself a heck of a lot better this way.
Whatever works for you, I hope your ride into the new year is kind, encouraging, and filled with remembering your own magnificence.

Hope this serves.
Love.

Shhhh

Shhhhhhhh.
Yeah, but I have to get the kids to hockey practice.
Shhhhhhhh.
Easy for you to say, you've been at this for years.
Shhhhhhhh.
I have to pay the bills first, then I'll...
Shhhhhhhh.
I could do this if I were thinner, less busy, healthier, richer, older, younger, blah, blah, blah.
Shhhhhhhh.
Yeah, but my head won't shut up.
Shhhhhhhh.
Yeah, but this is agony. I suck at this.
Shhhhhhhh.
Shhhhhhhh.
Shhhhhhhh.

The practice is not to wrestle my nutso mind to the ground.
The practice is to remember who I am underneath and beyond my mind.
Then mind can do whatever insane gymnastics it wants and I remain who I am.
That's what the shhhhhh means.

Just remember who you are- gorgeous, expansive, peaceful, whole, joyous, always-has-been-always-will-be you.

Hope this serves.
Love.

Shift Honestly Toward The Light

Gratitude, when it's forced, is like going to confession when you're a kid:
I'm sorry for the way I treated my parents and my brothers and sisters (note the lack of specificity here, because I was ten, for god's sake, not to mention good hearted and essentially innocent), I'm sorry for not doing enough around the house, etc., etc.
I don't remember much more. I apologized for my entire existence every week by making things up in as vague a way as I knew how, and he - on behalf of He - responded by suggesting I say 32 Hail Marys and we'd be good to go, pure as white, biblical lambs until next week's inevitable sins.
What it did was teach me not to be myself.
I pretended I had sinned, I pretended to be sorry, and I pretended to believe in absolution via recitation of meaningless (to me) words.
I'm not dismissing the act of confession, by the way. Done sincerely and with understanding, it's probably fabulous and uplifting. Cleansing, maybe.
It was, nonetheless, ridiculous for me at the time.
I SO envied a junior thug and heathen named Steven Larkin, who refused to traipse across to the church with the rest of us on confession day. He's going to hell, I thought, but he's going honestly.
(Yikes. I'm chatty this morning.)

So. Forced gratitude: I'm so freaking grateful for this illness, this poverty, this lousy relationship, this rejection, etc. are similar to fake confession in that the reality underneath is that I am not grateful but I'm supposed to be.

This takes us further away from ourselves and from truth.

What to do, what to do?

The point is to shift honestly in the direction of love and something lighter.

So.

I am glad the sun is shining. I'm glad that my coffee is delicious, in my favourite mug, and that we haven't run out of cream.

I am glad that I'm not forcing myself to be what I'm not today.

I am glad for the fact that, even on bad days, good things happen.

I'm glad that I'm better than I used to be at seeing good things.

I'm glad that I have a skill set that helps me turn a day around.

I'm glad for anything that makes me laugh.

I'm glad for being honest, hopeful, and trusting most days.

This is the process. It doesn't take much, does it?

Before long, a space opens up in which I can breathe more fully, and things feel lighter, easier, clearer, closer to the truth of who I am.
Honest shifting.
Practice this for a while, and maybe we end up being grateful for everything, even the tough stuff.

Hope this serves.
Love.

Shifting to Yes

There's a kind of reorienting that helps sometimes, when I realize I've been saying no in subtle ways: disagreeing with what is, with the people around me, with my best self.
And it's not like I'm smacking people over the head - sometimes this disagreement is only happening in my thoughts, as tiny bits of resistance, but this resistance is powerful when it becomes the tune I'm humming all day long.
The opportunity, then, is to shift to an open, generous yes, to see that life isn't happening to me, but through me.
To move from push, pull, manage, I don't think so, to observe, serve, allow, yes, yes, yes.
In this shift I fall backwards into the arms of Love.

Hope this serves.
Love.

Sometimes Breath Is a Refuge

Sometimes breath is a refuge.
Don't know how to deal with the crazy-ass chunk of life in front of you? The thing that feels bigger than you and insurmountable?
Bring your attention home, into this one breath which is whole, spanking new and yet familiar, our built-in reminder that beginnings and endings are the way it goes, our reminder of how important it is to receive and then let go, our affirmation that we can drop everything and the universe will continue to breathe us.
This breath is at least as real as whatever story I've been stuck in.
I can do this conscious breath once and change my chemistry.
Twice and I hardly recognize who I was twenty seconds ago.
Three times and the story in front of me begins to lose its power.

Hope this serves.
Love.

Speak Up (Imperfectly)

If you shut up or warp yourself into something weeny and untrue every time someone raises an eyebrow, disagrees with you, criticizes you, ignores you, laughs at you, or strums your unworthy chord in any other way, you will never know the sound of your own voice.
You break your contract with the universe when you choose not to be who you are.
So speak up. Do it imperfectly because that's the human way. Stop apologizing for that.
And stop waiting for your parents, your lover, your boss, your kid, your wish list of admirers to be okay with this.
It isn't the world's job to have faith in you or give you permission to be yourself.
They have enough to do trying to feel worthy themselves.
This is between you and You. You and Love.

Hope this serves.
Love.

Starting The Day

Starting the day with your mind in charge is resigning yourself to being a wind-up toy. You'll be exhausted and sick of the noise by noon. From this place, there are problems to solve, there are cranky moods, cranky bodies, cranky relationships. Lots of striving, pushing, me vs you stuff.
This is seeing the world with the wrong eyes.
Breathe yourself back home. Bring your attention inside until you are here, now, the singular point where you as a human meet the entire universe. Open and release here.
This is your point of power. This is your divinity.
Start here.
Through these eyes the world is completely different, isn't it?

Hope this serves.
Love.

Stay Sane Around The Suffering of Others

Stay sane around the suffering of others.
This doesn't mean be unloving.
It does mean that your suffering doesn't help them.
(This magnification of suffering is what most news media attempts to do: create distress by reporting distress.)
Remember who you are and who the sufferer is underneath the suffering.
Keep your eye on Love.
This is how we serve.

Lots of love your way.

Stop Taking Your Mind Back

Stop taking your mind back to your "mistakes".
We're going to get some things "wrong" every single day of our lives, sometimes in cute, tiny ways, and sometimes in ways that turn our guts into huge, seething balls of macramé.
It's life. Let it go. Looking back makes you small and gives you a bad neck.
Be here, be open, be as big as the sky.

Lots of love in your direction.

Stop Thinking For a Second

Stop thinking for a second.
Being here is a miracle.
Stop worrying/planning/hoping/pushing/guilting for a second.
Being here is a miracle.
Don't clutch at the thoughts that go by. Let them go.
It's a miracle being here, now.
Enjoy that for a moment.
Let it sink in.
A worthy practice over coffee on a Sunday morning.

Hope this serves.
Love.

Striving

Sometimes we feel that without driving our lives with goals, timelines, and self-flagellation, we'd lapse into apathetic drifting. We'd sit watching tv all day, drooling beer and saliva into a bottomless bag of chips. Question this.
Maybe when we drop personal striving, life goes on anyway. Maybe we get the chance to witness life pouring through us in fuller colour than before.
Maybe choices get made when they need to, paths get chosen, and we move forward without the planning, worrying, and weighing of pros and cons.
Our actions become inspired instead of feeling like push every day.
This may discourage the mind, which loves the striving, but it is a welcome relief to heart, which has known all along that the striving creates a beige life at best.

Hope this serves.
Lots of love.

Surrender Isn't So Hard

Surrender isn't so hard. It's not as though my mind has been a fantastic leader all this time. Most days, I'd be better off letting my socks run my universe. Let go. See what happens.

Lots of love.

Surrendering To The Great Loving Whatever

I don't know anything more important than a morning practice that reminds us of our wholeness, our worth, our connectedness, of the importance of leading with the heart.
Why get out of bed before softening the hard bits, dropping the heavy judgements and the suffocating fears.
It's imagined junk, all of it.
It does not serve.
Surrendering to the Great Loving Whatever is what makes us sane. It ends the relentless ego mantra of 'I am not enough, you are not enough, this is not enough'.
Why not accept that you are loved, that your life is in excellent hands, and that you can relax your forehead and your jaw for a few hours? Can we try that and see if things work out?
I'm paraphrasing Bill Murray from a recent interview with Charlie Rose (it's fantastic, if you get the chance): He said, what an incredible feeling, first thing in the morning, to say to the great whatever, I'm awake, what would you like me to do today?
Imagine the lightness of that.

Hope this serves.

Love.

Take Any Problem You Have

Take any problem you have, or any bit of suffering.

For a moment, drop everything that's happening anywhere else. Drop spouse and kids, friends, enemies, work, every injustice in the world, all the oily ducks and poisoned fish, politics, global whatever, planets, stars.
(If you can't drop something, you now know what holds you hostage.)
Now drop everything that came before now: your entire history, every story you have, every belief, every opinion. Just for the moment.
Drop everything that might come after this minute. Drop your goals, plans, your fears, your certainties and uncertainties.
Now drop your name, your age, your sex, your body, your health. Drop every thought that shows up.
Just keep dropping.
(You can pick all of it up later.)
What's left?
Are there any problems left in this place?
We say no, but it isn't real, it isn't true, this empty place.
Is this place less real than the busy-headed, problem-filled spot you were in before?

Drop everything and sit with what remains.
Maybe this is how you find your way home.

Hope this serves.
Lots of love.

The Answer To Nervousness

The answer to nervousness is to be here. Stop projecting worst case scenarios.
The answer to being overwhelmed or too busy is to be here. In this moment, you do not have 7,000 things to do.
The answer to anger or resentment is to be here and now. Let go of what happened this morning or a year ago or when you were twelve.
The answer to worry is to stay here and now. You can't keep people safe by worrying. Adding bad energy never, ever helps.
The answer to how to live well is be here, now.
When we stop squeezing the hell out of this moment with our corrosive, habitual thinking, an openness shows up. A kind of natural joy begins to flow through.
With this comes trust, patience, peace.
You remember what it is to feel light.
This is the practice.

Hope this serves.
Love.

The Challenge Is to Practice

The challenge is to practice staying here and now in a way that feels nurturing and encouraging rather than it feeling like a bull fight in a hurricane.
One way to do this is delight in every moment you're here.
Another is to stop beating yourself up over the moments you are distracted or carried away by thought or emotion. Tormented self-flagellation, as attractive as it is sometimes, is not the point.
An exercise:
Be immersed in making your coffee while making your coffee. Let it be a full, complete experience.
Leave your to-do list out of it for now.
Forget multi-tasking for a moment.
This is enough practice to last thirty years.
And if your life crashes to the ground at some point during those thirty years, you'll look for and find a deeper practice.
(The joke is that while making coffee, we're planning the thing we're doing at ten. And at ten, we're thinking about how this meeting is killa boring and we'd rather be at lunch and at lunch we're wishing we didn't have to go back to work but we have to to meet the payments on the hummer, and back at work we're exhausted and then we go home and try not to think about the day. We have a few drinks and try desper-

ately to let go for one second. HA! What a crazy sitcom! No wonder we're looking for something a little saner.)
One breath at a time. xo.

Hope this serves.
Love.

The Morning Shift

I love the morning shift that happens some days.
You wake up, your head hurts a bit, it's still cold outside, you're a bit worried about a couple or seventeen things, you're not any smarter or braver or more talented or more beautiful or younger than you were yesterday. And the dog is needy. Not to mention your spouse. And that #%#%ing right hip.
The world's a mess. Students shot in Kenya, big oil wrecking the planet. All the Big, sad, scary stuff.
This can happen in my head in the first three minutes.
Trashy place, this head.
Then I make the decision.
Not to be in denial and not to fake my way toward anything.
I make the decision to genuinely appreciate something.
I'm glad for coffee. I'm glad for the very fresh air that circulates through this cottage we live in.
I'm very glad for the fire that my lovely man just started in the wood stove.
(At the start, I don't even use the word 'grateful' if it feels too smarmy. Is smarmy a word?)
I am SO glad that spring is coming.
I'm glad that my right hip is improving and that there are a thousand possibilities for more improvement.
This body teaches me a whack about acceptance, pa-

tience, trust, hope, strength, the management of energy.

I'm glad for every student who hasn't been shot. I'm glad my heart breaks for the ones who were. I'm glad the world cares about that.

I understand the big oil thing is complicated. We love to scream about it but we also love to live in big houses and drive mammoth SUVs and eat food that's shipped across the planet for us. I'm glad we care about living well and I'm glad we care about what's happening to the planet. I have great hopes that we're finding our way forward to good solutions.

My little dog is sort of permanently lame now so yeah, she's needy, but she's an excellent friend.

I have a body that breathes.

I have a heart that loves to be open and connected.

And I have choice. Every single day I have choice about leaning in the direction of thanks, trust, generosity.

Every single day I can choose to be here, now, where all is good. Better than good.

This shift changes everything.

#beafoolforlove
#thepowerofthanks

Hope this serves.
Love.

The Practice is To See the Squirrel

Don't take your neurotic days too seriously. It's not like who you really are has gone anywhere.
And don't buy the idea that it's hard to get from neurotic here to peaceful there.
Ego is like a squirrel on crack dancing in front of your face, doing its best to convince you that the world is unsafe and that you are not enough.
You've heard that story a thousand times and believed it too often.
The practice is to see that there is a squirrel!
Let the rodent chatter on.
Your job is not to shut the squirrel up, but to listen/feel beyond it, beyond the superficial in-your-face stuff.
The squirrel will get less noisy when you stop feeding it.
Peace is here. Take one breath and be here.

Hope this serves.
Love.

The Problem Isn't The Problem

Something to consider:
The "problem" isn't the problem. Our persistent gathering of resistant energy around it is the problem. That energy is what creates havoc in your body and attracts similar lousy energies to your thinking, your feeling, and your circumstances.
As an experiment, drop the problem completely. Now watch how often you find your mind trying to pick it up again - reviewing the right/wrong/he/she-was-an-asshole arguments, picturing worst case scenarios about that discomfort in your gut that must be a massive tumour, remembering the crappy feelings from yesterday's news about pipelines, unsolved murders, etc.
(Even if these feelings are 'justified' - even if you have the tumour and your spouse is a shmuck and painful things happen in the world - it doesn't mean it makes sense to maintain your suffering around these things. It's one thing to suffer and another thing to suffer your suffering. Might as well spend the day picking at your own scabs and sticking forks in your eyeballs for all the sense this makes.)
What can we do about this?
We can accept our craziness and choose to be free in this moment. Let it be and let it go.

(Someone will be thinking, but you SHOULDN'T IGNORE THE TUMOUR! It's funny that we're afraid we won't act if we don't suffer. Do you not think we could listen to our instincts about our bodies, our relationships, and our planet without the suffering? Would we not act out of love?)
Let it be and let it go.
This is a worthy practice.
We are so bizarre and so gorgeous.

Hope this serves.
Love.

The Whole Shebang

When you throw your unimportant self into the fire and die to love, even the painful bits - illness, conflict, abandonment, grief, sorrow, 'death' - become gorgeous.
This will remain an idea until we do it.
How do we do it?
Forgive every single thing. Let the hostages go.
Drop your ideas about what you need to be happy and be happy.
Drop your ideas of right and wrong and be free.
See Love/Beauty/God in the set of eyes across from you even when you can't stand the set of eyes across from you.
Just accept that Love is the point of all of this. The whole shebang.

So happy to be in this together.
Huge love.

The You That Is Unbroken

Is it possible that you don't need healing, fixing, self-improvement, personal development?
Maybe the personality can use all of that. In fact, maybe the personality is addicted to all of that because it thrives on the idea of being broken or less than.
Can you find the you that is unbroken? The you that watches this oh-I'm-so-flawed-but-at-least-I'm-working-at-it dance?
Be obliterated by your own beauty (which is to say the beauty of everything) just once and you will never be completely fooled by your personality again.

Hope this serves.
Love.

This Illusion of Control Is a Funny Thing

This illusion of control is a funny thing.
We resist/push/manage our circumstances, our bodies, our work, our age, our relationships, our "purpose". We're taught that this is what life is, changing ourselves and our circumstances in order to climb the ladder, to be happier, to live a worthwhile life.
(The chronic dissatisfaction around discovering purpose is such a win for ego. You can't throw a rock without hitting someone who lives an entire life gnashing their teeth about whether or not they're living their purpose. Gnashing this #%€£ing glorious moment away.)
What about throwing all of that away and just being here?
Being fully here and now without the gnashing sounds absurdly trite, doesn't it?
Here, now: It'd fit on a bumper sticker or a coffee mug. The criticism is that it's brainless. It's for people who can't handle real thinking, real problems, real planning and goals and action steps, real solutions, real life.
Well. Gnash away if that feels right.
For some of us, a light goes on and it begins to look as though no amount of striving, no accomplishment, no

amount of control will feed the real hunger, the real homesickness.

I'm not saying this change of perspective is best or should happen for all of us.

I can say a different life begins when this light goes on.

When we are here and open, something - life, LIFE - happens through us instead of to us or from us. It's like, ohhhhhhhhhh! I'm not driving this thing! If I'm not driving, how do I do this?! Do I let go? Can I let go?

This surrender - this surrender of ego, this giving up of a mind-dominated life - isn't passive. It isn't resignation.

It's a massive, committed choice to be here and present despite the ego-driven world yelling that what IS is not enough without your control. That you are not enough.

That you are stagnating and losing if you are not striving. That if you stopped striving, your life would stop. There's a cosmic joke in here somewhere. It's like we're drops of water in an ocean and we don't know about the ocean. So we bust our asses trying to turn ourselves into fancy cars or houses because we want to be powerful and elegant and meaningful. It'll never work. And drops of water are kind of pathetic on their own, so it's no wonder we're trying our best to turn ourselves into something else.

You have to surrender at some fundamental level in order to experience yourself as OCEAN, to feel the power of that, to understand that this is your nature. There's nothing trite about this kind of surrender. It's huge. It's the biggest thing you'll ever do. This surrender is the most profound kind of activism.
If you make this choice, you'll know you're home before long. You'll remember, somehow.
Some days I feel like apologizing for going on so inelegantly and ineptly about this.
But every morning I wake up thinking nothing else matters.
So.

Hope it serves.
Love.

This Is All There Is

Funny to think that most of our suffering comes from attempting to be there instead of here:
I would rather be wealthier, in love, smarter, more fit, less fat, in better friendships, doing more fulfilling work, not in this conflict with you, better at everything I do, further along in my career, in the body and face I had ten years ago, where I hope to be ten years from now, more energetic, more useful in the world, etc.
This pulling and pushing sets up a kind of tension.
It makes the foundation of your house wonky so that your doors won't open and everything starts to crack.
It makes music that's off because the harmonies and time signatures are all wrong.
It feels uneasy.
It's even funnier, when we're striving to be somewhere else, to realize that there is no there there.
This is not a bumper sticker sound bite.
It's the truth. We're striving and creating all of this tension for something that doesn't exist.
This - now - is all there is. This is the point of power.
Which can depress the hell out of you if you have been saying no to the life in front of you and investing your hopes for happiness in a fictional future or a long gone past.
The real peace, the non-fiction joy, comes from being willing to be right here, right now. Accept it. Open to

it. Make this moment worth it. Make this moment the gold standard of your life. Breathe yourself into right now.

This is the sweet spot. This is the real music, this is the true, natural foundation. This is what opens doors. If this doesn't feel true, ignore it.

If it does feel true, enjoy.

Hope it serves.
Love.

Three Ways to be Free

Three ways to be free:

1. Tell the truth about who you are - in the next thought, the next sentence, the next interaction. Be conscious about it. (Some of this will be pretty, some won't.)
2. Live that truth. Act on it. Be brave. (Some of this will be pretty, some won't.)
3. Now let the people around you - kids, friends, spouses, ex-spouses, critics - do the same. Let them go. They are not here to make you feel better, and they are not here to live according to your values. (Oooooh, some of this will feel pretty, some of this will feel messy/gross/terrifying.)

In every moment we are choosing approval, safety, and control, or choosing freedom.

#heartchoosesfreedomeverytime

Hope this serves.
Love.

Throw Away Your Separateness

Open up.
There's something so excellent about realizing we're part of a whole, that we're tiny drops of water in the huge ocean of all that is.
We're pretty ridiculous and powerless on our own except in a kindergarten way of posturing, comparing, defending, competing, needing to be better than, needing to be right.
And we're astoundingly powerful when we accept our ocean-ness.
We're in this together whether we like it or not.
Be humble and be great.
Throw away your separateness. It doesn't serve you anymore.

Hope this serves.
Love.

To The Young Woman on Cash At The Grocery Store

I was just in the grocery store, buying paprika and chili powder. It was my second time in this store in less than an hour. Most of the cashiers are wonderful in this place, the kind of women (why always women on cash? Another chat for another day, maybe) who notice you're there for the second time.
"You, again! You can't get enough of us!"
I was next in line and had my paprika and chili powder on the conveyor belt thing when I heard a man yelling, "Hey! Heyyyyy! HEY!!!!!!!" By the third hey, it was LOUD.
I turned around and saw Robert running toward me. Robert was a patient in my clinic when I had a clinic. This means I haven't seen him in almost three years. Robert is intellectually challenged or whatever the inadequate terminology is now. He processes the world in a different way than what the experts call normal. And his life, because of this, is challenging in different ways than mine.
He's a big, beautiful hunk of human flesh and he was running toward me with three years worth of enthusiasm.
When he smacked into me and wrapped his arms around me I started crying and saying, you're so beau-

tiful, you're sooooo beautiful, and he yelled, thank you, thank you, THANK YOU.

That was it for dialogue, but we were at it for about five minutes. Then he just put me back down on the floor and walked away.

I was felled by it, the way anyone would be, seeing a long lost love. I wasn't wailing at this point, but there was still a steady flow of salt water falling down my face.

The young woman at the cash, who could not possibly have missed this whole thing, said, while looking over my shoulder, "Excuse me, do you need bags?"

"What?"

"Do you need bags?"

Oh, man, it made me sad.

Here's what I want to say to her.

Honey, you just witnessed two people being felled by love right in front of you. Do not hold your doors closed. It will kill something in you and in us if you stay closed.

It's also very likely that the next person in line has been felled by fear (of the price of these groceries, for instance, or of cancer or of the pressure at work) or loneliness or delicious lust or gratitude or some other force.

What a crime not to open the doors of your gorgeous self and be with us. Sad for us and sad for you.

What, you think your job is ringing up the price of paprika?

Honey, your job is to be in Love with us. The paprika, the cash register, and your bright green uniform are props. They are excuses to practice knowing who you are.

Love and openness are your real job.

That's what I want to say to her. She was too beautiful – we all are – to forget this.

Let's be felled together. Just falling over with love all day long. Why not?????

Thanks to all the free and not-yet-completely-free cashiers out there, and to beautiful Robert.

And thanks to you for the conversation.

Truth and An Undefended Heart

Today, tell the truth to yourself and to the world and do your best to live with an undefended heart.
Let the universe do the rest.

Hope this serves.
Love.

Two Minutes of Being Here, Now

There's a kind of low level, habitual suffering that adds up to chronic, dull, dense energy.
First thing in the morning:
A little more sleep would have been nice.
Coffee. Where's the coffee.
Man, the snow is deep out there.
Yikes, I can still feel that lower back.
Wish that project funding would show up today.
So-and-so is ruining the environment.
Wish I weren't so lazy.
etc.
It's a list of minor judgements and complaints. Objections to what is.
It adds up to a foggy, resistant energy, 100% of it generated by our minds, not by actual circumstances.
It's just ego doing it's crabby thing.
I doubt that mind/ego ever stops this.
But we have choice.
I can see this fog for what it is and snap out of it.
It's possible to see those thoughts and not own them or be owned by them this morning.
It's possible to focus instead on the miracle of breathing in and out.
I mean, really, if you were witnessing your breathing for the first time, would you not be amazed by it?

Who's doing this thing, this contraction and expansion that allows me to be alive at all this morning? When I let it all be new, which only requires that I be here and now, I look across the bed and think, o my god, there's another human BEING in this bed! There's a doggo BEING lying across my LEG! And I have EYEBALLS to see this with! And oh my god, YOU have EYEBALLS that see it all COMPLETELY DIFFERENTLY.

And there's a WORLD outside the window! A WORLD! Look at SNOW! Are you telling me that those SNOWFLAKES outside are unique? And that they're there because of how this PLANET is moving around this SUN!?

What the hell! Why are we not all freaking out about this?

(What a massive, cosmic joke, that all of this is going on while we complain about having to shop for tonight's dinner.)

All this miraculous stuff going on in every moment. Two minutes of being here, now, and I laugh at myself for ever complaining.

The fog lifts and I remember.

#complainingisadrag
#youaremorebeautifulthanthat

Hope this serves.
Love.

Underneath The Snotty Stuff

You hear people say, love what is, and you think, oh, god, right, okay, and you look at your thighs, your face, your job, your deadlines (what the hell is that word about?), your health, your cranky relationships, and you resolve to do your best to Love That Horrid Thing.
It can be easier than this. Don't resolve. Don't work at this.
You've been carrying something heavy that isn't yours. It's a used Kleenex, except that it weighs a whack more than that.
It served a purpose, all this junk, but there's no law that says you have to carry it around with you every day and forever.
Say yes somewhere inside and beyond your trained-by-your-family/culture/workplace/religion mind.
Drop all of it, drop yourself, drop everything.
Love this, whatever this is right now. Do love, be in love, be Love.
It's like flying, it's so free.
It is who you are underneath all the snotty stuff.

Hope this serves.
Lots of love and courage your way.

Until We Surrender

Until we surrender, it's all about how to manage this life more effectively, how to reshape the world around us. How to push away the stuff we don't like, how to more effectively collect the stuff we do like. Discipline, control, striving, goal setting and achieving.

You know all those quotes about how your life will run you if you don't run your life, the posters with pictures of eagles telling you what it takes to be a leader.

This approach is wonderful for a while, isn't it? It gives us a sense of power and certainty. Maybe safety, too. I want this, I do what it takes to have it, I feel good in the world.

If all of that brings you the greatest joy and inspiration, keep at it.

On the other hand, you may tire of it at some point, even if it has worked well for you.

You may sense an emptiness underneath.

It's possible that you may some day want to throw all of that into the fire of something greater. (You will feel it in your chest and gut if this is true.)

When the day comes, you may want to bow down and surrender to the great energy that created you, whatever that is.

You may see your imagined control as a ridiculous head game.

You may see that outside, right now, buds don't control their unfurling, ecstatic crocuses their blooming, ice its melting.

You may sense, at some point, that it's the same for you.

Life pours through you. Life is breathing you. The most natural thing you can do is let go and adore the feeling of Life Pouring Through You.

Then life is no longer about managing, pushing, climbing.

You live it. You celebrate it. You feel it instead of thinking it.

Is this scary? Of course it is.

Do you sense the truth of this?

If not, carry on.

If so, welcome.

Hope this serves.
Love.

Walking By Broken Glass

There's something funny about the way we defend our bad feelings:
I can't help it, we say. He doesn't listen to me and that makes me feel bad. I'm so miserable every time I think about it.
My mother was critical, so I feel unworthy any time someone is the least bit critical.
I didn't get the last two gigs I auditioned for. I feel untalented and unworthy. It makes me reluctant to try, to express my creative self at all, it sucks the courage right out of me.
These thoughts and feelings are there, what can I do???
You can ABSOLUTELY do something.
Change your perspective.
If, while walking down the road, I see piles of broken glass, I do not pick them up and rub them into my skin or stuff them in my mouth. I do not come back to the broken glass again and again, and I do not obsess about its painful potential. Why would I do any of that?
Every time I see a pile of glass, I walk by. I continue walking because I love walking, I love the day, there are a thousand beautiful things going on, and I don't love the feeling of glass being rubbed into my face. This is so obvious, isn't it??

Somehow, we forget that we have the power to focus. We practice focus all day long by focusing on stuff that makes us feel joyous and courageous and free or on stuff that makes us feel like shit, to put it bluntly.

Most of the world is rubbing glass into skin. (This is how a lot of media, marketing, religion, politics, education and health care work.)

Make a different choice. The moment you think a crap thought, notice what you're doing, put it down, and walk by. Choose instead to notice your lungs breathing, sunlight making shadows on that building over there (sunlight! shadows! buildings!), another day to choose, another day to be alive.

People say, you're being naive! You Pollyanna! You're in denial!

Isn't it strange that choosing the pain of rubbing glass into your skin is called facing reality while choosing to look at leaves changing colour, clouds moving overhead, your dog's gorgeous face, someone's kindness, or the seven shades of lichen on that rock is called denial?

Choose your focus. This is the practice. It isn't any harder (people say, oh god, I'll try but it's SO hard) than leaving broken glass on the road.

We do it by leaving the sharp stuff one pile at a time.

Hope this serves.

Love.

Want To Change The World Right Now?

We go on about wishing we knew more about our purpose on the planet, wanting to serve, to be useful. Want to serve in a way that changes everything over the next hour?
Hold eye contact for as long as you can. I'm not talking about stalking anyone. Just give it five seconds, seven if you're feeling reckless. See someone's insides. Allow yourself to be seen.
This would be enough to change everything. It'd generate miracles. And it's certainly enough to scare the hell out of most of us.
If you want more, go on:
Listen fully, not just until you know what you'd like to say next. Listen until long after the other guy is finished. Leave a space. See what happens. See how it feels.
Speak honestly and fully when you do speak. Speak from a truer place than usual. Be willing to speak from an unprepared place, discovering the truth as you go. See what happens. See how it feels.

#wanttochangetheworldrightnow?
Let me know how it goes.

Hope this serves.

Lots of love.

Want To Change Your Life?

Want to change your life?
Stop doing what you don't believe in.
Stop following.
Find out what is true for YOU and throw yourself into that.
(I can't imagine anything lonelier or more dispiriting than living someone else's beliefs and values. Someone else's life.)
All day long, the universe whispers: follow the joy, follow the joy, follow the joy.

Hope this serves.
Love.

What Would Love Do?

We have this central core of love. Constant, aware, still, quiet, alive, peaceful.
And then we have personality and ego layered on top. Striving, overshooting, planning for worst case scenarios, hanging on to bad memories, easily offended, arrogant one second, self-deprecating the next.
Slowly but surely, we move toward the core being master and the ego being servant.
One of the key words here is slowly.
Here I am, at 53, and I still have quite a thick asshole layer. (Maybe you want a different name. This one works for me.)
This is the layer of ego that is irritated with my lovely man this morning because I'm grieving the death of a good friend this week and somehow I can't sit quietly with the sharpness of grief. Instead, I slice away at the surprised people around me like a weed whacker gone mad. It makes no sense but it happens.
I resent the success of others when I'm in this place.
I'm competitive and driven by imagined scarcity.
I say unthinking, hurtful things to other gorgeous humans.
(This is the way I feel at every party.)
I feel certain I don't belong.
I get horribly critical, as though making you wrong makes me right, makes me better than you.

I get needy. (Line up and tell me I'm gifted, loved, necessary. Don't talk about yourself or that oil spill. In fact don't talk at all once you've told me I'm wonderful. Let me talk. Make me feel fascinating. I'd never say this out loud, but that's what goes on in Needyville.)
I sound terrible on the flute, my writing stinks, my imagination disappears and takes my confidence with it.
Do you know this gig?
This is immature and exhausting. It's the gross part about being human.
And all the meditating in the world hasn't eradicated it. It does thin it out, it does, but I wanted it gone.
The only thing I can do when I'm operating in threatened, reactive asshole mode is to
STOP.
Stop and observe.
Don't judge.
Breathe. Bring my attention to breath.
Stop running from whatever discomfort I'm feeling.
Turn to face my discomfort. Open my arms to it. Open my slammed shut heart.
Sit compassionately with my own grossness.
And when things calm down a bit (they always do when compassion is allowed in), I can ask:
What would love do here?
Sit with that for a bit.
Sometimes love would be quiet.

Sometimes love would express my grief more clearly to my lovely, bewildered man.
Sometimes love would listen deeply to you.
Sometimes love would take a nap or get out for a bit of air.
Sometimes love would find a sense of humour about this being human business.
What would love do?
Follow this question home.
This is the practice of being human some days in my neck of the woods.

Hope it serves.
Love.

Whatever The Difficult This Is

Whatever the difficult THIS is - the thing that has bumped up your suffering - the relationship, the bad news, the not enough money, the rejection, the internal state of anxiety or depression or anger or fear - stay open to it.
Look it straight in the eye, turn your body toward it, and keep an open heart. Be here with it. Breathe into it. Relax into it.
Then respond.
In this way, we accept what is and act from the best place in the universe.

#consciousnessasactivism
#braveheartschangeeverything

Hope this serves.
Love.

When Angry, Afraid, Envious, Judgemental

When angry, afraid, envious, judgemental:
If you want relief, shift your perspective.
(It's interesting to note how often we don't want relief. Sometimes we revel in the feelings, don't we? Momentarily, anger, judgement, etc. can make us feel powerful. This is excellent until it's not. When it stops feeling excellent, this shift of perspective will feel good.)
Instead of being inside your anger and consumed by it, try seeing it as a storm passing by in front of you. This storm is sort of seductive. It resonates with stormy thoughts from you (he's a bastard, she's a liar, they betrayed me, abandoned me, ridiculed me, ignored me, the world's going to hell, she doesn't love me, I don't have enough money to be safe or happy, that ache in my back is a tumour, blah, blah, blah).
If you identify with these thoughts and allow them to hang out they will bring others just like them. Before long, you're humming with every serial killer/Ebola story on crap TV. Before long, your neighbour is a serial killer and you have Ebola.
You are inviting the storm to stay instead of passing by.
You are growing the storm.
If instead, you DECIDE not to identify with these thoughts, if you say no thanks to them and let them

go, over and over, the storm passes by because that's what storms do.
It's so useful to remember that you are not the anger or the fear.
You are the one watching the storm.
You are something more grounded, more central, and far more peaceful than the storm.
There's a kind of waking up that happens when we remember this.
In this way, our practice creates a pathway from victim-y insanity to freedom.

Hope this serves.
Love.

When I Picture The Universe Talking To Me

When I picture the universe talking to me, she says things like:
Have a little faith, sweet heart.
You're doing so well.
Yeah, sometimes it feels hard, but even hard times can be delicious in moments. This too shall pass.
You are loved.
Even when you struggle to like yourself, YOU ARE LOVED.
Remember that comparison is the thief of joy.
Remember that all crappy/destructive/cruel choices come from suffering.
All things are possible.
The best things arrive in ways you could not have thought up on your own.
Breathe.
Open your heart.
I'll catch you when you fall.

Does the universe really talk like this?
I have no idea.
But I feel happier, braver, more powerful, and more generous when I live like this.
I see a better world.
I create a better world.

I live in love with all of it.
This is the point.

Hope this serves.
Love

When I've Mastered Being In This World

When I've mastered being in this world but not of this world, I may be able to look with love on the shitty stuff: sexual crimes, environmental crimes, financial disparity, the suffering around addiction, animal cruelty, the way humans justify killing humans in war, the relentlessness of me vs you, right vs wrong.
With enough perspective, it may all look like colours in a tapestry. I trust, based on my weeny human experience of it, that judgement falls away with practice and love.
I'm looking forward to more of that perspective.
Until then, while this stuff shreds my insides, I can practice:
- leaning in the direction of gratitude for good things, simple things. A body that works well enough, heat for the winter, my kids, my dog, my curiosity, a heart that can still be opened by sad and happy things.
- compassion for my own feelings. Staying in the room and open with my hurting heart is a major accomplishment.
- compassion for the other guy. Trusting that we're all doing our best to find our way home. This only becomes real for me, i.e. beyond being a good idea, when I feel full compassion for myself.
- taking care of my energy. Choosing not to drown in

the stuff that makes me suffer. Choosing to feed myself with what makes me sane. Knowing what my heart needs and giving that to myself.
- acting from love instead of fear, especially when it comes to the causes that come with suffering. I can carry placards with love. I can hold a picture of what we'd love to see happen to the planet. I can trust that change is possible and that we're all in this together. In this way, now is all I need. It's good. It's full. It's enough. (Which is just as well, because it's the whole shebang.)
#lovingwhatis

Hope this serves.
Love.

When Someone Is Making Me Nuts

When someone is making me nuts, it is never, ever the truth that they need to change.
The issue is mine and all mine.
The sooner I see this, the sooner I get to truth and powerful solutions, the sooner I get to peace, the sooner I am free again.

Hope this serves.
Love.

When Thinking Is Compulsive

When thinking is compulsive, we're out of sync with ourselves and the nature of the universe.
(Omg, I have no clean shirt for today and I'm late and I wish I were on holiday or rich or doing something I loved or felt loved or felt like my work mattered more or knew what I wanted out of life or could be myself without wrecking all my relationships or okay forget all that I just wish I could find a #%£¥ing clean shirt.)
Our nature is not so nuts.
Our nature is the back and forth of inhale-exhale, be-do, active-receptive, moving-still, outward-inward. When we're hijacked by thinking, ego, the outside world, or dissatisfaction with this moment, we're missing the restorative half of the cycle.
When we learn to stop thinking, to let our minds rest, we create balance and a kind of space inside.
This space or openness is the fertile ground of peace, creativity, balance, sanity, compassion, and an understanding of connectedness. It's heaven.
So to make this practical, consider not starting the day with your to-do list, not starting the day with the news, or with the one thing that pisses you off (e.g. no clean shirt).
Consider starting the day with an easy awareness of this day, this moment, this room, the air in this room, this breath, this body.

Bring your awareness home.
There might be a compulsive resistance to this at first. Don't fight that. Just practice. Five minutes, maybe.
Before long, you begin to feel a yearning underneath, a homesickness for the stillness, that makes this practice easier.
Soon you'll look for this whenever you become nuts, whenever the world feels nuts.
You'll know that the answer is to bring yourself home.

#peaceisherejoyishere

Hope this serves.
Love.

When This Mouth Opens

When this mouth opens, it's either love speaking
or it's fear speaking.
And no matter what happened five minutes ago,
the next time I open my mouth I get to choose
again.

Hope this serves.
Love.

When You're Thinking It To Death

The universe is living you.
Stop wresting with the details.
You'd go mad trying to thought-manage your breathing all day long:
You know my inhalations aren't bad - they're too short most of the time and they're shallow but I've got a successful breathing coach helping me with that. I'm as good at inhaling as most of the people around me. I'm a better inhaler than you are.
But my exhalations are crap. I'm just a lousy exhaler. All through school my teachers told me just to pretend to exhale 'cause I was disturbing the kids around me. And I've missed out on a lot of opportunities because of my exhaling. I'll never be an opera singer now. I'm afraid that if I don't get my ass in gear with exhalation, I won't even be able to retire when I want to. And how will I take care of my kids if I'm failing at 50% of this breathing thing?
Maybe your life will happen beautifully without your think-y management, just like your breathing does.
Be here, now. Live this moment without thinking it to death.
See what happens.

Enormous love in your direction.

Where Your Art Comes From

When it comes to your creativity, to expressing your one and only self in any facet of your life, you can make choices:
You can lie about your self and who you are in order to not rock boats, to be accepted by the people you're trying to please.
This is suicide.
You can not lie, exactly, but rather keep quiet, stay mute rather than risk attention, disapproval, loneliness, poverty, etc.
This is just a quieter suicide.
You can honestly skim the surface of your mind and heart and say out loud to the world, This Is Who I Am. This takes guts because some people will love this level of you, some will completely reject your voice, and some will say, meh. This demands that you care more about your life than the opinions of others.
Or you can go even deeper. You can purposefully walk over and over through the closed doors in your mind and heart, become completely lost and sometimes terrified, and be willing to feel your way around in the darkness until you discover something new about your self and the world.
You can express from this place.
This takes a kind of persistent courage in every cell, every neuron, every heartbeat.

This is where your art comes from.

Hope this serves.
Love.

Which Part of You Leads?

How strange that we see gratitude and compassion as lightweight, kindergarten, Hallmark-y sentiments that are sweet until the going gets rough, at which point we'd better apply our minds to goals, action steps, real work. Time to grow up and take care of business.
I get that this is a useful phase: Mind first.
But how long does it take - how many accomplished goals, how much stuff accumulated, how much 'material freedom' - before we know, deeply, that this ain't it? That mind solutions have not resolved mind's fear?

Both this moment and this LIFE are about choosing which part of you leads.
Mind as leader creates one life that is about safety and winning.
Heart as leader, mind as servant creates another. This one is about surrender and connection.
If I choose heart, gratitude and compassion become my work, my practice. And holy god, they take muscle some days.
Finding real gratitude when all I can see is stuff that pisses me off is a HUGE choice.
Finding compassion for people who scare the shit out of me is a HUGE choice.
Finding gratitude and compassion for myself is toughest of all some days.

Heart first takes constant courage.
And it changes everything.
It creates a world I want to be a part of.

Hope this serves.
Love.

Worrying

Worrying = focusing my very powerful energy on bad outcomes for myself and for the ones I love.
Do we need to discuss this or should we just slap ourselves in the head and move on?
#putyourenergywhereyouWANTit
#wearefarmorebeautifulthanthat

Hope this serves.
Love.

Yippy Squirrel Talk

Something to consider:
The first words out of my mouth rarely, rarely have anything to do with truth or love. The first noise out of my mouth is usually yippy squirrel talk.
Take a breath. Take another breath. Speak when you remember who we really are.

Lots of love in your direction.

You Are Not The Squirrel

Even when we hear simple things, like "let it go, let it go", our minds jump in like adolescent squirrels. (Whaddayamean let it go?, easy for you to say, I let it go before you we're born, I'm too afraid to let it go, I'd quit my job if I let it go, I'd start yelling and never stop if I let it go, only peacenik loser slobs talk about letting it go, what happens to my retirement savings if I let go, what happens to my kids, what happens to my nine o'clock meeting, I'd just turn on the tv, eat chips and drink chocolate milk if I let it go, okay, okay, I'll try it for a second, okay, that didn't really work, see, I told you so, so this isn't for me, ...)
All of this in about three nanoseconds, in the mind. So forget about answering when you hear something like "let it go".
Maybe sitting with it at a slower, deeper place, living with and through these questions, is what we want.
Let mind do its crazy answering. Just don't get caught up believing you are the squirrel.

Lots of love.

You Are the Ocean

There's something really funny about our resistance, about our allegiance to our minds.
We're like drops in the ocean, saying, "I don't know about this ocean thing. It's so hard. I get glimpses some days, and I have a kind of hunger for it, but I'm afraid, and my life gets in the way. Maybe I'll get it some day, you know, when the kids move out and I can take a bit of time off work.
For now, I'll read about the ocean when I have time, and listen to other drops who look like they've been to the ocean. Wish I understood this. Wish I could be at the ocean right now, but you can't just give it all up and be ocean, you wouldn't survive, and what would happen to my relationships with all the drops I love? Wish I could really believe in the ocean, but, man, it's hard, you know?"
Stop.
YOU ARE THE OCEAN.
You don't need time and you don't need to read any more.
YOU ARE THE OCEAN.
You can stop telling yourself otherwise right now. Or realize that your "I am a solitary drop" gig is not the truest you.

Every time you hear it, and you'll hear it four billion times a day, you can remember it isn't you.
YOU ARE THE OCEAN.
(This isn't about leaps of faith or believing what anyone else says.
In your heart of watery hearts, you know whether or not this is true.
I'm just suggesting we keep looking, keep asking, keep our real eyes open.)

Lots of love.

You Belong In The Middle of The River so Quit Clinging to the Shore

We want to be out in the middle of the river, moving with the current, feeling the power of it, enjoying the buoyancy, trusting it, feeling its potential.
Living our potential.
Something about the river resonates with the most alive thing inside ourselves.
We see rare people doing it - walking into the water and swimming out into the current. It looks crazy but exhilarating. It looks free.
But we're scared #%*¥less of letting go.
So we cling to the shore, scared of the wee bit of current we do feel around our feet: holy god, that big current will never carry me, it'll never pay my mortgage, it's a nice idea, I like reading about it but I'm not strong enough to do it, I'll drown, or maybe I could build a massive life jacket first and take swimming lessons for 47 years and keep hanging onto this rock I'm clinging to, that's the responsible thing to do, and those people swimming out to the middle are reckless, irresponsible fools, anyway. Lots of shore-clinging experts say so.
This clinging will never create a joyous life. You are afraid and training yourself to stay afraid.
Joy comes from letting go into to what you know (You KNOW) you are.

And we say, I hear this, but I can't let go! I can read about it, and I agree, but I can't stop clinging. I don't know how to do that and be okay.

For a while, it'll be okay to talk about it and read encouraging quotes while you cling.

This won't satisfy in the end.

You belong in the middle of the river.

Hope this serves.
Love.

You Choose Your Thoughts

You choose your thoughts.
Sure, habitual, scary, discouraging, heavy, unsupportive thoughts come by, having to do with old crap or imagined future crap.
But we have absolute choice when it comes to hanging onto them or letting them go in this moment.
We say, what can I do? I drop them and they come back.
You are more than your weeny thoughts. Understand the power you have!
(Do not make this an opportunity to crucify yourself for your 'flaws' or to defend them. That's an ego grab that does not serve.)
Let the junky thoughts go. Let them go again. Let them go again.
Replace them with another thought. A better thought. One about the hope of relief or gratitude for the fact that we can breathe or the fact that we have a planet that spins through space in such a way that we are here at all.
Or drop your thoughts altogether and be here, now, in this breath, where everything is okay. Because everything is okay in this moment without your thoughts. Keep doing this.
This is the power of choice. This is the practice.

We build thought patterns from the thoughts we choose, and from those we build a life.
This is not about blame, it's about responsibility and potential. It's about management of energy and stepping into your power.
#putdownyourweenyness

Hope this serves.
Love.

You Know These Moments of Being Felled

The challenge in talking about this 'being awake' thing is that words don't cut it. Words absolutely can not describe the wordless.

What we're all trying to with inadequate black squiggles and spaces is point toward the enormity of what IS, toward what we are and have always been, fully and hugely, underneath the yappy, tight, visually impaired immaturity of the ego.

I know very few people who aren't aware of their own central spark of connectedness to the whole. (I know a lot of people who are uneasy about attaching that spark to anything religious. I might be one of those.)

When we see something beautiful - great art, the night sky, the movement of water, the geometry of snow flakes, your kid's face - something recognizes beauty. We don't just see it, we recognize it. Something in us knows, because something in us IS that.

Despite the limits of language, the words of others (and their art, their music, their silence, their loving eyes) have often stirred something in my gut that re-oriented me in some essential way.

The great teachers (thanks, thanks, thanks) have a way of opening something inside, some insanely deep well of knowing that we are more than we think, that we are energy more than matter, that by directing our

energy/attention we accomplish more than any mental or physical pushing can hope to do, that what we feel and think affects everything (this is activism), and that we are really, truly one and in this together.
They look at us and we know we are beautiful and whole, somehow.
You know these moments of being felled, obliterated, woken up, humbled, inspired, reminded.
As soon as we touch this beauty, this wholeness, we're in awe.
And oh my god, awe is where we belong.
Lean toward this today.

Hope this serves.
Love.

You Only Have to Open the Littlest Bit

You only have to open the littlest bit and the universe goes wild.
Open, open, open.
(Say yes, say yes, say yes.)

Hope this serves.
Love.

You've Got To Step Up To Receive

You've got to step up to receive.
If you feel unworthy of what you're asking for, it isn't going to work.
You're trying to mix energies that don't mix.
Become the clear, knowing, deserving receiver. Step up to that. Step into your divinity. Be open and strong here. And know that you are a part of the inhaling and exhaling of the universe.
This sounds flaky, I know, but the moment you feel it working and see it working, it becomes realer than real.

Hope this serves.
Love.

Your Creativity Is Your Life Blood

Your creativity is your life blood.
And every single one of us is filled with it, whether we're acting, painting, singing, writing, making dinner, deciding what to wear, deciding what words and gestures to use in love or conflict, when choosing books, films, TV, while daydreaming, while recalling the past or imagining the future, while letting our energy FILL and be filled with this moment.
(Also when gossiping, blaming, worrying, dwelling on guilt, shame, or fear, which are all creativity that hasn't found a more powerful channel yet.)
So take notice of your language and energy around it. It matters.
Stop saying you're not creative. It isn't true and it does not serve you except to keep you living under a rock.
Be brave with your creative instincts. They may not look like anyone else's. That's sort of the point of creativity. It's the spark that happens when the universe meets the uniqueness of you.
Slap perfectionism in the head every time you meet it. It paralyzes. Read Anne Lamott on shitty first drafts. This applies to every creative act.
Do what you can to stop caring about the opinions of others. This may be a lifetime's work but it's the only way to find your own voice instead of relentlessly imitating voices you think will be palatable to the people

whose criticism you're most afraid of. (Who are those critics, by the way? And why the hell would we choke off our life blood for the sake of another human's critical thoughts?)

Critics do not belong in the same ring as creators. (Somebody said this before me.) Tattoo that on your heart.

Dream about what you'd do creatively if you knew you were completely loved and that everything were guaranteed to work out. This is good for courage.

Stop swallowing popular opinion. Question it.

Tell the truth about who you are and what you want. Energy is mucked and incoherent until we tell the truth. Tell yourself the truth even when it's uncomfortable and it will get easier to tell the world.

Everything you put out into the world is open to criticism - your feelings, your choices, your art. That's the way it is.

So often we put out a false version of ourselves in order to fit in or to look better than what we sense we are underneath. Stop this.

Cultivate the dance of thick skin thin skin. Lean toward nakedness.

Be yourself. Commit to this. There is no point in being here otherwise and the entire world is waiting for your voice. This is not an idea. Feel it. Know it.

Hope this serves.

Love.

Your Mind Wants To Screw Everything

It's helpful to remind myself once in a while that my mind is not who I really am.
It's a tool, like a screwdriver - useful when I use it, completely mucked when it's using me.
It's a screwdriver that wants to screw screws. This is okay.
But it wants to screw everything.
It wants to screw a to-do list for today, it wants to choose the food I eat, determine my career, call the shots in my relationships, keep me attached to my past and afraid of my future, and judge my self-worth.
More than anything it wants to prevent peace in this moment.
If you let your screwdriver design the house you build, you will never be happy with the house.

#payattentiontowhoyoureallyare

Lots of love your way.

Your Pyromaniac Days Are Over

Kindergarten love flaps its way through relationships, creating and putting out emotional fires.
Lots of drama queen suffering with this one.
It's possible we're addicted to this suffering for a while. It's so satisfying, in a crazy way, to start a fire, or to pour gas on one that's been started already, and then to race in and out of the burning building, shouting and screaming, blasting power hoses in the other guy's face.
Grown up love focuses instead on the thing that can't burn down. It means looking through the fire to the other guy's heart.
This one's more peaceful, more powerful, and possibly more fun.
Your pyromaniac days are over.

Hope this serves.
Love.

Thanks

Thanks so much for reading.
Thanks to those of you who asked for a collection of these morning writings and to those of you who were already collecting them in manilla folders on your bedside tables.
Thanks to all the great teachers - the human lanterns - who remind us who we are and of the life that is possible.

Feel free to join us at DrKristinShepherd on Facebook, @kristinwonders on Twitter, or at kristinshepherd.ca

Made in the USA
Charleston, SC
21 November 2015